OXFORD WORLD'S CLASSICS

GROUNDWORK FOR THE METAPHYSICS OF MORALS

IMMANUEL KANT (1724–1804) was born in Königsberg, the capital of Eastern Prussia, and spent his entire life as a writer, teacher, and academic in his home city and its environs. He studied philosophy and the natural sciences at the university between 1740 and 1746. He spent the succeeding years as a house tutor and, subsequently, as a private lecturer, publishing a number of substantial essays and treatises on scientific and philosophical subjects throughout this period. Kant finally became Professor of Logic and Metaphysics at the University of Königsberg in 1770. Over the next ten years, which Wilhelm Dilthey described as the 'silent decade', Kant radically revised his earlier ideas and developed an entirely novel conception of the proper method of philosophy, which culminated in his epochmaking *Critique of Pure Reason* in 1781. He extended his 'transcendental' approach in the *Critique of Practical Reason* of 1786 and the *Critique of Judgement* in 1790, the work which Kant himself saw as completing the entire 'critical enterprise'. Throughout the 1790s Kant also produced an abundance of dense contributions to fundamental questions in ethics, politics, history, and religion. Kant retired from lecturing in 1796 and died at the beginning of 1804. The *Groundwork for the Metaphysics of Morals* and his *Critique of Judgement* have both greatly influenced the philosophical tradition and remain central reference points for the contemporary discussion of the nature and value of Kant's thought as a whole.

CHRISTOPHER BENNETT is Professor of Philosophy at the University of Sheffield. He has published widely on topics such as criminal justice and punishment, forgiveness, moral emotion and moral agency. In the history of philosophy he is particularly interested in Kantian and post-Kantian approaches.

JOE SAUNDERS is Assistant Professor of Philosophy at Durham University. He studied at the University of Canterbury in New Zealand, and completed his PhD at the University of Sheffield. His research focuses on ethics and agency in Kant and the post-Kantian tradition, but he also has interests in media ethics and the philosophy of love.

ROBERT STERN is Professor of Philosophy at the University of Sheffield, where he has worked since 1989. He is a Fellow of the British Academy. He has published extensively on Kant, Hegel, and transcendental arguments, as well as on accounts of moral obligation. A collection of his papers on Kant was published by Oxford University Press in 2015, under the title *Kantian Ethics: Value, Agency, and Obligation*.

OXFORD WORLD'S CLASSICS

*For over 100 years Oxford World's Classics have brought
readers closer to the world's great literature. Now with over
700 titles—from the 4,000-year-old myths of Mesopotamia to the
twentieth century's greatest novels—the series makes available
lesser-known as well as celebrated writing.*

*The pocket-sized hardbacks of the early years contained
introductions by Virginia Woolf, T. S. Eliot, Graham Greene,
and other literary figures which enriched the experience of reading.
Today the series is recognized for its fine scholarship and
reliability in texts that span world literature, drama and poetry,
religion, philosophy and politics. Each edition includes perceptive
commentary and essential background information to meet the
changing needs of readers.*

OXFORD WORLD'S CLASSICS

IMMANUEL KANT

Groundwork for the Metaphysics of Morals

Translated with an Introduction and Notes by
CHRISTOPHER BENNETT,
JOE SAUNDERS, AND ROBERT STERN

OXFORD
UNIVERSITY PRESS

OXFORD

UNIVERSITY PRESS

Great Clarendon Street, Oxford, OX2 6DP,
United Kingdom

Oxford University Press is a department of the University of Oxford.
It furthers the University's objective of excellence in research, scholarship,
and education by publishing worldwide. Oxford is a registered trade mark of
Oxford University Press in the UK and in certain other countries

First published as an Oxford World's Classics paperback 2019

Impression: 7

Published in the United States of America by Oxford University Press
198 Madison Avenue, New York, NY 10016, United States of America

British Library Cataloguing in Publication Data

Data available

Library of Congress Control Number: 2019948775

ISBN 978-0-19-878619-1

Printed and bound in Great Britain by
Clays Ltd, Elcograf S.p.A.

Links to third party websites are provided by Oxford in good faith and
for information only. Oxford disclaims any responsibility for the materials
contained in any third party website referenced in this work.

CONTENTS

INTRODUCTION

'[T]HE present groundwork is nothing more than the identification and vindication of *the supreme principle of morality*' (4:392).[1] In this way, Kant makes clear his two central intentions for the *Groundwork for the Metaphysics of Morals*: first of all, to uncover the principle that underpins morality, and secondly to defend its applicability to human beings. The first task is the focus of the initial two sections of the text, while the second task occupies the third section.

Despite the apparent modesty of the book's title, therefore, in claiming to offer a mere 'groundwork' or preparation for the full-blown 'metaphysics of morals' that Kant hoped to write later,[2] this is still a formidably ambitious text. For to have correctly specified the fundamental principle underlying all moral action, and to have vindicated its application to human beings, would be no mean feat. The originality and profundity of Kant's attempt to achieve such significant goals explains the attention that this short work has attracted since its publication, as readers continue to debate whether he has succeeded, and indeed how his project is best to be conceived.

This project is ambitious and intriguing because Kant gives fresh answers to traditional questions about the fundamental nature of morality and its place in human life. One central question concerns the *content* of morality, that is, answers to practical questions like 'What does morality say that I should do in this situation?' or 'How does morality say that I should live?' Secondly, there are questions about the *authority* of morality, of whether morality is something that genuinely binds us (and

---

[1] References to Kant are to the volume and page number of the Akademie edition of his works. The translation of the *Groundwork* below has the Akademie page numbers in the margin of the text.

[2] The *Groundwork* appeared in its first edition in 1785, and was revised for the final edition in 1786. It thus appeared a few years after the first edition of Kant's ground-breaking contribution to theoretical philosophy, the *Critique of Pure Reason* (first edition 1781, second edition 1787), and was shortly followed by the *Critique of Practical Reason* in 1788 and *Metaphysics of Morals* in 1797 that are promised in the Preface to the *Groundwork*. For translations of the latter texts, see Immanuel Kant, *Practical Philosophy*, translated and edited by Mary J. Gregor (Cambridge: Cambridge University Press, 1996).

if so how), or whether its purported force is just an illusion; and if it does have force, what place we should give moral considerations in comparison to other kinds of considerations that might interest us, such as our own welfare or the welfare of those we care about. Thirdly, we might ask about the *reality* of moral standards: for instance, whether they exist in empirical reality like tables and chairs (or whatever our best science tells us are the basic constituents of the world), or whether they are products of the human mind and human societies, or whether they are neither empirically real nor human inventions, but have a reality of some third type. And fourthly, we will want to know something about *human nature*, so that we can understand how, or whether, morality connects to human understanding and agency, and hence whether human beings are either incapable or (at least sometimes) capable of acting on moral standards, if they do indeed have some reality.

At the end of this Introduction, we will consider Kant's position in the light of these four questions, but first we will provide a summary of the work, in order to orientate the reader through this compressed and challenging masterpiece.

Identifying the Supreme Principle of Morality

Given that the text is structured round the two tasks of first *identifying* the supreme principle of morality, and then *vindicating* it, we see most clearly what Kant was trying to accomplish by considering each of these questions in turn.

For Kant, there are two related reasons why he needs to find the right supreme principle of morality. Firstly, various inadequate candidates for this principle have been proposed by philosophers, theologians, and others, and these proposals are potentially influential; and so secondly, unless this principle is correctly identified, our moral lives may be jeopardized. Moreover, Kant does not think it is an accident that all efforts to identify this principle prior to his own have ended in failure. As he makes clear in the Preface, one reason others have gone wrong is that they have conducted their investigation in a way that is too empirically grounded—for example, by basing it on claims about typical human emotions, or about the social rules needed to enable us to live together as the creatures we are. Kant argues that any such approach must be inadequate, because morality does not just apply to *us* and thus follow from our empirical circumstances and nature, but rather applies to *all rational beings*, which means that we need to proceed in a way that avoids all such empirical considerations—and hence is a priori (cf. 4:389).

Kant then offers us not one but two such a priori (or non-empirical) routes of investigation, both of which purport to converge on the same place by arriving at the same supreme principle of morality, but by taking somewhat different though complementary paths. The first route (which is found in Section I) takes us from a broadly common-sensical conception of what it is to have a good will, to the principles by which this will must operate; and the second route (which is found in Section II) takes a more philosophically informed starting point concerning the nature of practical reason, seeking to correct how this was misunderstood by the 'popular moral philosophy' of Kant's day. Both of these routes are said to be a priori as they proceed *analytically*, by analysing the very concepts of the good will and practical reason respectively, while they then show *synthetically* that the principle arrived at in this manner is the one we actually use in our moral thinking (cf. 4:392). Overall, therefore, Kant's method in trying to identify the supreme principle of morality is to ask: on what principle would the good will (in Section I), or the fully rational agent (in Section II), decide to act?[3] For if we can arrive at an answer to these questions, we can ascertain what that supreme principle must be, as this will be the principle that such agents use to determine their actions. We can now turn to follow Kant down each of these paths of inquiry.

GROUNDWORK SECTION I

The *Groundwork* begins by explaining why it makes sense to start our search by investigating the nature of a good will and the principles on which it acts: for, Kant argues, a will that is good is the only thing which is 'good without qualification', and which has an 'absolute worth'. Kant claims that it is unconditionally good because, on the one hand, the good will can never be complicit in the bad (unlike otherwise admirable traits

[3] And cf. 4:437, where we arrive at the point of convergence of both inquiries: the first inquiry, beginning from the good will, is identified in the first main paragraph; and the second, beginning from rational nature, is identified in the following few paragraphs.

of character, for example the courage that makes a person into a better thief); and on the other hand, other capacities and circumstances (such as intelligence and wealth) are only of positive value if allied with the good will. Moreover, Kant claims the good will is of *absolute* worth because its value is not dependent on what it actually accomplishes or brings about, for a will can be good even if its purposes are wholly frustrated by 'step-motherly' nature (cf. 4:393–4). One might think otherwise, perhaps, if one thought nature has given us reason in order to accomplish the purpose of achieving our happiness, so the will is good only if that is the result; but this, Kant argues, would be a mistake, as if the role of reason were merely to lead us to attain happiness, nature would have been better off just giving us instinct instead (cf. 4:394–6). Kant therefore takes himself to have vindicated the special status of the good will, and shown why it is a promising place to start his investigations, while equally being a concept that 'already dwells in natural sound understanding' (4:397), which is why he can claim to be proceeding here on the basis of 'common rational knowledge'.

However, for reasons that Kant does not really explain at this point, but which become clearer later, he now switches from the *good* will to the *dutiful* will, which (he says) 'contains that of the good will, but under certain subjective limitations and hindrances; however, far from concealing it and making it unrecognizable, this rather brings it out by contrast and makes it shine more brightly' (4:397). This switch is based on a thought which Kant discusses more fully in Section II (cf. 4:412–14): to beings like us—who, unlike God, do not have a *holy* will—goodness always takes the form of appearing as *duty*. This is because beings like us do not simply act on the good, but must be *compelled* or *obliged* to act against their countervailing inclinations. Thus from here onwards, rather than asking what principle the *good* will would act upon, Kant now focuses instead on what principle a *dutiful* will would act upon; and for that, we have to know more about what it is for a person to be genuinely dutiful.

Kant begins by arguing that such a person must not merely *conform* to their duty simply because they feel so inclined, but rather must act *from* duty. In order to establish this, he considers two types of case in which inclination might be involved, arguing that in each of these types, the agent is wrongly related to their duty, and hence they gain no moral credit from their action—where he acknowledges that the second type is the most controversial (and so it has proved). The first type is where one's ultimate inclination is self-interested, but that interest is nonetheless best served by acting in line with one's duty: such as a shopkeeper who treats their customers honestly, not because they see that this is the right thing to do, but because they recognize that this will help their business. Kant takes it as obvious that this shopkeeper is not a genuinely dutiful agent. However, he then gives three examples of actions of the second type, where it is less clear that there is anything wrong with the inclination itself: a person acting to preserve their own life out of the *self*-regarding inclination to do so; a person acting to benefit others because of an amiably disposed *other*-regarding inclination; and a person acting to make themselves happy simply because they are naturally inclined to see this as good. Nonetheless, Kant argues, in each case, there is still something wrong in treating these individuals as properly dutiful agents, as we can see when we contrast them with the examples of a person who feels no such inclination in these cases, but who *still* acts as they should by recognizing the relevant act as their duty. Claiming that only then does the person have genuine moral character, Kant takes himself as entitled to conclude that a properly dutiful person, who has real moral worth, is one who acts *from* duty, and not from an inclination that is merely *in accordance with* duty (cf. 4:397–9).

Having established this first proposition about the dutiful agent (though without explicitly numbering it as such), Kant now moves on to what he identifies as a second proposition: 'an action from duty has its moral worth *not in the purpose* that is to be attained by it, but rather in the maxim according to which it is decided upon' (4:399). Kant takes himself to have already shown that the moral value of an action cannot come from the end that the agent desired to achieve or actually achieved—for example, to treat their customers honestly—for the agent could achieve this end without acting from duty. Rather than the value coming from any material principle which derives from desires and inclinations, he argues that it must come from a merely *formal* principle instead.

But then the question arises, if the dutiful agent acts on a formal principle, unrelated to their desires and inclinations, what is it that motivates them to do so? This question leads Kant to his third proposition:

'*duty is the necessity of an action out of respect for the law*' (4:400). That is, a dutiful action is done independently of the person's desires and inclinations, and so must instead follow simply out of respect for the law under which the action falls. In feeling this respect, the agent views the law both with reverence and awe, as what stands above them and strikes down their self-love, but also as having a value that draws them to it. The law can therefore appear as alien to us and at the same time as that in which we are realized, and so as something we impose on ourselves; and thus respect is akin to both fear and inclination, though it is not reducible to either of these feelings or sentiments, but is a unique kind of attitude of its own, and so serves a special motivational role in the life of the dutiful agent.

Having argued for this third proposition regarding dutiful action, which he says is the conclusion from the first two, Kant now takes the final step in his search for the supreme principle of morality in this section. From what has been said so far, we know that a dutiful agent is one who acts on laws which they take to hold independently of their desires and inclinations, and which are capable of inducing reverence in that agent. It thus follows that the principle on which such an agent acts is to consider whether the way in which they propose to act, and thus the maxim under which their action falls, is capable of being a law of this kind and hence holding universally, as a law must. Hence, by considering what duty involves, and what principle is adopted by the dutiful agent to guide their actions, we have arrived at the supreme principle of morality: 'I ought never to proceed except in such a way *that I could also will that my maxim become a universal law*' (4:402).

Kant then proceeds to try to make good on his claim that in this section he has been working in accordance with 'common human reason', by offering an example which illustrates how we implicitly use this principle in our moral thinking, so that while we may not have been conscious of it until now, in fact we have always already had the principle 'constantly in view' (4:402). The example concerns someone making a false promise, who can see that they have a duty not to do so by asking themselves whether this could hold as a universal law; for they will realize that if false promising were allowed, then there would be no promising at all, as no one would trust anyone else sufficiently to make this possible. Thus, it will be evident to the person that false promising fails to meet the principle and so should be rejected as a maxim, for 'as soon as it were made a universal law, [it] would necessarily destroy itself' (4:403). As agents, therefore, all we are required to do in order to follow our duty and hence act morally is ask ourselves, 'can you also will that your maxim become universal law? If not, then it is to be discarded; not because of the prospect of some cost to you or others, but because it cannot serve as a principle in any possible universal lawgiving, for which reason compels immediate respect' (4:403).

Finally in this section, Kant raises a potential worry for his project: namely, if (as he argues) the principle he has identified is indeed the 'compass' that always already lies in the hand of common human reason, and if this compass is really so easy to operate as he suggests, why is philosophy needed in this area at all? Indeed, might not philosophy just serve to corrupt the 'fortunate simplicity' of ordinary moral understanding, and lead it astray (cf. 4:403–4)? Kant clearly feels the weight of this worry, and acknowledges that the need for philosophy in practical life is much less immediately obvious than it is in the theoretical sphere to which he had devoted his previous philosophical writings, such as the *Critique of Pure Reason*. Nonetheless, he wryly notes of our practical dispositions: 'Innocence is a wonderful thing, but sadly it is so hard to preserve and so easy to seduce' (4:404–5). That is, while duty can ask us to act against our needs and inclinations, and does so on the *basis* of reason, we can also come to reject this duty, as it may equally seem to go *against* reason to neglect our needs and inclinations in this manner. This can give the appearance of a conflict or 'natural dialectic' within practical reason: while moral action can look supremely rational from one perspective, it can look supremely *irrational* from another. This can then be sufficient for common human understanding to start to doubt the validity of our duties, and so be seduced away from the path of morality, not by philosophy, but by its own uncertainty regarding whether morality is genuinely rational. This is therefore why a second section of the *Groundwork* is needed, to look more closely at practical reason itself, and to show that even beginning from this more philosophical starting point, we will still come to the same place as we did in Section I when we started from common rational knowledge, and so will converge on the same supreme principle of morality. However, as we will see, Section II leaves certain loose ends unresolved until Section III, so the full defence of morality against this 'natural dialectic' will not be accomplished until then.

GROUNDWORK SECTION II

Kant begins Section II by underlining that he has been operating in an a priori rather than an empirical manner thus far, in that his argument has not depended on any given *examples* of dutiful agents to the principles on which they might act, but rather on the *concept* of duty and what it is to be a dutiful agent as such. In this way, Kant argues, he can bypass several difficulties that plague a more empirical approach—such as the problem of plausibly identifying any such examples, which arises partly because we can never be confident that people are really as morally upright as they may appear, and partly because it is hard to see on what basis one might identify such agents without already using the supreme principle of morality to do so. Likewise, he argues, his approach avoids many of the dubious empirical assumptions made by 'popular moral philosophy' which seeks to ground morality on claims about human nature, or happiness, or our moral sentiments, where all Kant needs to appeal to instead is his a priori investigation into how reason operates in the dutiful agent (cf. 4:406–12). However, as we saw at the end of Section I, there is some question over how precisely reason works in this context, so to get further with this issue we must abandon 'popular moral philosophy' and its hopeless search for examples, and instead turn to metaphysics, in order to 'trace and clearly present the faculty of practical reason, from the general rules by which it is determined right up to the point where the concept of duty arises from it' (4:412). At this stage in the text therefore, after several pages of polemic and preamble, Kant's investigation into practical reason begins in earnest.

Kant's first step is to argue that while 'everything in nature works according to laws', only beings with a will can consciously *follow* laws, by using their practical reason. In agents whose reason determines their will without fail, they will simply act on the laws presented to them by reason. However, in agents also afflicted by inclinations as well as reason, these laws will be seen as *overcoming* or *constraining* these inclinations, and will thus appear to the agent as involving *necessitation*, whereby the agent is compelled to follow what reason commands, and so act contrary to their inclinations. Thus, Kant argues, for agents with inclinations that go against reason, the principles on which they act will take the form of *imperatives* which are expressed by an 'ought': 'Such imperatives say that to do or to omit something would be good; but they say it to a will that does not always do what is represented to it as good' (4:413). As a result, therefore, Kant distinguishes (as we noted previously) between, on the one hand, a *holy will* that always does what is represented to it as good, and so is not constrained by any imperatives, and, on the other hand, less perfect wills such as our own, for whom what is represented as good appear as commands of reason issued to beings like ourselves who have inclinations that could diverge from reason.

Kant then draws a fundamental distinction between two imperatival forms: *hypothetical* and *categorical*. A hypothetical imperative says that you ought to act a certain way, or that an action is good, as it will get you what you want, where the 'ought' only applies if you want to attain this end—for example, if you want to become a pianist, you ought to practise the piano. Acting on such imperatives appears to be self-evidently rational, as if you will the end, then it seems you must will the means (although, of course, in reality we do not always act rationally in these respects). A categorical imperative, by contrast, tells you how you ought to act *regardless* of what it is you desire—and Kant thinks that the imperatives of morality all fall into this camp. Thus, for example, morality tells you that you ought not to lie, irrespective of how this may affect your own interests or concerns, but simply based on 'the form and the principle from which the action follows' (4:416). As a result, categorical imperatives do not ground the bindingness of the 'ought' on the way in which it will help you achieve goals set by your desires.

However, whilst hypothetical imperatives seem pretty unproblematic, unfortunately categorical imperatives can appear deeply puzzling, in a way that brings us back to the 'natural dialectic' raised at the end of Section I. For, if acting on a categorical imperative, and thus acting on a moral imperative, does not serve as a means to satisfying one's desires, what can make it *rational* to act on any such imperative? Isn't it only rational to follow hypothetical imperatives, and thereby satisfy one's desires—and if so, doesn't this put the rationality of morality itself in jeopardy? Thus, as Kant puts the puzzle: 'the only question that needs to be answered is without doubt how the imperative of *morality* is possible, since it is not a hypothetical imperative at all; and thus the necessity with which it is objectively represented cannot rest on any presupposition, as it does with hypothetical imperatives' (4:419). Putting it in his characteristic language, Kant identifies the difficulty as arising from its nature as a 'synthetic a priori practical proposition' (4:420, and note 8): namely, that something links the will to the action in a way that makes it rational (and so it is practical), but the link is not based on any antecedent desire and so is not derived from some empirical fact about the agent, as in a hypothetical imperative (and so it is a priori), but nor does it seem to be analytically contained in the concept of a rational agent that they act in this way (and so it is synthetic).

Somewhat alarmingly, at this point Kant tells us that to explain how such a categorical imperative is possible, and thus to vindicate morality, is something that needs to be deferred to the final section of the *Groundwork*, as 'this will require special and arduous toil', for which we are not yet properly ready and prepared. With this dark warning, Kant says instead that in what immediately follows he will take the possibility of such imperatives for granted, and instead see whether characterizing morality as involving these imperatives can help us confirm the outcome of the previous section regarding the nature of the supreme principle of morality itself, so that 'the mere concept of a categorical imperative may perhaps provide us with the formula that contains the only proposition that can be a categorical imperative' (4:420).

On this issue, Kant is much more immediately optimistic, and argues as follows: We now know that morality must consist in categorical imperatives, and that such imperatives tell us to act in ways which hold, not because of our contingent desires and inclinations, but as laws that apply to us universally and necessarily. It is therefore the case that the supreme principle of morality is *itself* a categorical imperative that instructs us to act on laws of this sort, and so tells us we must act on maxims that are fit to be such laws. In this way, then, via a different route, we arrive at a result that parallels the outcome of our inquiries in

Section I: 'Therefore there is just one categorical imperative, and it is this: *act only on a maxim that you can also will to become a universal law*' (4:421).

However, rather than simply letting matters rest at this juncture, and stopping at this point of convergence, Kant may seem to spoil his case by going on to offer *further* formulations of this supreme principle that apparently take us beyond what was said in Section I, raising the worry that rather than offering us *one* supreme principle of morality, Kant is, in fact, giving us several, thereby reducing his moral project to chaos. Nonetheless, as we shall see, while Kant does not explicitly address this worry, the way in which he connects together these formulations might be enough to assuage it.

The first of these variants takes the original formulation (widely known as the Formula of Universal Law, or FUL), and turns it into the following formulation (known as the Formula of Law of Nature, or FLN): '*act as if the maxim of your action, by your will, were to become a universal law of nature*' (4:421). Kant explains this transition on the basis that nature is itself law-governed, so if one is asking if one's maxim can become a universal law in accordance with FUL, one is also in effect asking if one's maxim could be a law that governs nature, in accordance with FLN.

Before giving his other variants, Kant then applies these first two variants to four key examples, which relate to four types of duty: duties to self and duties to others, and perfect and imperfect duties (that is, strict duties and those that allow for some latitude). Thus to the example of false promising discussed in Section I (which violates a perfect duty to others), Kant adds the examples of suicide (which violates a perfect duty to oneself), neglecting one's talents (which violates an imperfect duty to oneself), and the failure to care for fellow human beings (which violates an imperfect duty to others) (4:421–3). In each of these cases, Kant tries to bring out how the maxim that contravenes the relevant duty suffers from a fundamental incoherence or contradiction if we were to take it to be a natural law, either because we cannot even *conceive* it as such (which is the case for the perfect duties), or because we cannot *will* it as such (which is the case for the imperfect ones) (cf. 4:424). What this tells us, Kant suggests, is that given the incoherence of rationally conceiving or willing the universality of these maxims, and the fact that nonetheless we try to act on them, the concern with satisfying our own inclinations deceives us into thinking that the maxims do not hold *universally*, but just *generally* or on the whole, and as allowing for a few exceptions—exceptions such as ourselves. However, he thinks, this already shows our reason is corrupted when we take ourselves to be permitted to act on non-universalizable maxims in this way, as reason calls for proper universality, not mere generality.

At this point, therefore, Kant thinks he can legitimately declare himself satisfied with what has been achieved, namely to have successfully identified 'the principle of all duty', based on the characterization of duty as involving categorical imperatives. However, at the same time he sounds a note of caution, once again commenting ominously: 'But we have not yet got so far as proving a priori that there actually is an imperative of this kind—that there is a practical law, which commands simply of itself without any further motivating drive, and that following this law is duty' (4:425). Kant thinks that faced with this difficulty, philosophers have been tempted to take a more empirical route, for example by proposing some psychological disposition in human beings which might lead us to follow this principle; but this, he warns, can only lead to disaster, and the eventual corruption of morals, as such psychological dispositions will generally be linked back to our inclinations, and anyway, the principle of duty is meant to apply not just to human beings but to *all rational beings*, including those whose psychological make-up is unknown to us. Thus, Kant writes, the question before us is as follows: 'is it a necessary law *for all rational beings* always to judge their actions according to maxims which they themselves can will to serve as universal law?'; and thus what we need to show is that 'the law must already be bound up with the concept of the will of a rational being as such, in a completely a priori manner', for which a 'metaphysics of morals' rather than any sort of empirical inquiry is required (4:426), to help us understand how '*reason all by itself* determines conduct' (4:427), independently of our desires and inclinations.

In order to gain this understanding, Kant now argues, we must turn our attention to an issue that so far has not been brought into the discussion, and which will at the same time lead us to a further formulation of the supreme principle of morality. This issue concerns what can serve as the *end* or goal of acting on a categorical imperative: what it is that following the categorical imperative will bring about, and why this matters. This end cannot get its value simply because we desire it, as then it would generate a merely hypothetical imperative, rather than a categorical one. It must therefore have its value independently of any such desires, making it an end not just for us given our desires, but an end in itself, for all rational beings. For there to be the categorical imperatives that morality requires, therefore, their rationality must depend on there being such ends in themselves, which have absolute worth as such, rather than merely relative worth by being useful to us. But what is it that has such worth, which might form the ground or basis for such a categorical imperative?

Kant proceeds by offering an argument from elimination, stating dogmatically at the outset that the answer to this question is 'a human being and generally every rational being' (4:428); but then supporting this claim by arguing from elimination that no other possible options—namely things we produce because of our inclinations and needs, or non-rational products of nature—are suitable candidates. The former only have value because they satisfy our inclinations and needs, but that does not make them of absolute worth, as (Kant claims) we would sooner be without such inclinations and needs; and the latter (such as animals) can clearly be used as means (or so Kant assumes). All that is left to serve the role, therefore, are rational products of nature—namely *persons*, who are therefore said to have the absolute worth that is required, without which there could be no supreme practical principle of morality at all.

Moreover, once this is recognized, we can also see that another formulation of that principle is possible, namely the so-called Formula of Humanity (FH): '*Act in such a way that you treat humanity, whether in your own person or anyone else's, never merely as a means, but also always as an end*' (4:429). To establish that this is a plausible variant, Kant then runs through the same examples as before—of suicide, false promising, neglecting one's talents, and neglecting other people—to show how these cases violate this principle as well.

In addition, whereas previously we were just asking if our maxim could be a law of nature, we have now 'peopled' nature, so to speak,

by introducing a world that contains rational agents. This means that
the question raised by the formula of the law of nature can be modi-
fied to include such agents—so that now we are asking, could our
maxim be a law for them to adopt, where *as* rational agents, they are
conceived of as being capable of imposing such laws *on themselves*.
This then yields what Kant considers as the third variant (as he counts
FUL and FLN together as in effect the same), which is often
called the Formula of Autonomy (FA): 'the supreme condition of
the will's harmony with universal practical reason is the idea of *the
will of every rational being as a will that legislates universally*', so that
'[a]ccording to this principle, all maxims are rejected which are not
consistent with the will's own universal legislation' (4:431). Finally, in
thinking of ourselves as legislating our maxims to other rational
beings in this way, and asking if as rational beings they could adopt
such maxims as their own, we are in effect thinking of ourselves and
others as a community of beings who are treated as ends in themselves—or what Kant calls 'a kingdom of ends', giving rise to
a modification of the Formula of Autonomy known as the Formula of
the Kingdom of Ends (FKE): 'never to perform any action except
one whose maxim could be a universal law, and thus to act only on
a maxim *through which the will could regard itself at the same time as
enacting universal law*' (4:434). By treating one's fellow moral citizens
in this way, Kant argues, one treats them as possessing not mere *price*,
but as possessing *dignity*, the dignity that is appropriate to them as
beings with absolute worth.

Thus, in the end, Kant finds a way to group together the various
formulations of the supreme principle of morality that he has identified, and has offered us a way of seeing them as more than a collection of quite disparate formulae. Kant argues for this coherence by
suggesting that FUL/FLN give us the *form* of the principle, FH
gives us the *matter*, and FA/FKE fit these both together in a satisfactory manner (4:436), while then going on to give a helpful summary
of his whole argument (4:436–40). In this way, Kant takes himself to
have achieved his first main goal, of identifying the supreme
principle of morality, while showing that this is a principle with several different aspects.

Finally, in this section, Kant turns to criticizing his rivals and opponents, who have offered *other* and competing accounts of what this principle should be. Kant's aim is not just to show that those competing principles are mistaken, but also to diagnose *why* his rivals have gone wrong; and as the subtitle on 4:441 suggests, he thinks this has happened because they have operated with a *heteronomous* conception of the will, while his own account treats the will as *autonomous*. To see the will as autonomous, for Kant, is to see the will as choosing to act not because it is governed by some object of desire, but rather because the maxim of its action can be rationally endorsed, by being seen to be universalizable, so that rather than being 'the slave of the passions' (as Hume famously declared it ought to be),[4] reason is their master. However, Kant argues, other moral philosophers have not seen the will as autonomous in this way, but have assumed that it is in fact heteronomous, and so sided either with the empiricist Hume in assuming that the will bases its choice on its inclinations or feelings directly, or (if they are more rationalistically disposed) on some rational ideal to which it is said to be attracted. Either way, Kant argues, '[w]hether it rests on inclination, or on representations of reason, it is only hypothetical imperatives that are made possible by this relation: I ought to do something *because I want something else*' (4:441); but as we have seen, this misses out the essential, categorical nature of moral requirements.

Kant discusses two wrong-headed principles of morality that arise from each of these approaches—an empiricist approach which either thinks the principle is that we should pursue our own happiness, or that we should satisfy our moral sentiments; and a rationalist approach which either thinks we should pursue our own perfection, or should follow the perfection of God's will. In all these cases, Kant argues, these principles are morally dubious, unable to specify any concrete action, and to be satisfactory would require further grounding on a principle like his own. However, of course, he thinks the fact that moral philosophers have fallen into error in this way is scarcely surprising, given that the right approach is only available once one has adopted the autonomous rather than heteronomous conception of the will that he is proposing, and thus correctly grasped the distinction

---

[4] David Hume, *Treatise of Human Nature*, Book II, Part 3, Section 3, edited by P. H. Nidditch (Oxford: Oxford University Press, 1978), 415.

between hypothetical and categorical imperatives on which his breakthrough in this area has relied.

In this way, then, Kant takes the aim of Sections I and II to have been successfully completed: the correct supreme principle of morality has been identified, and shown to be superior to any of its rivals. However, as we have seen, throughout this discussion some further fundamental issues and questions have been postponed, and Kant reiterates this in the closing paragraph of this section, requiring us to go beyond the 'metaphysics of morals' which was attempted here, to offer instead a 'critique of pure practical reason', in order to finally explain and understand how it is possible for a rational being to act on a universal law for which it has no further non-moral motivation or interest. Until this synthetic a priori claim can be vindicated, the possibility remains that morality is a mere 'phantasm' (4:445)—it is this crucial issue which we require the 'special and arduous toil' of Section III to resolve.

Vindicating the Supreme Principle of Morality: Groundwork *Section III*

Just as Kant has warned us, Section III turns out to be hard work. It is dense, and the various parts of it are both hard to understand on their own, and difficult to piece together. But it is also ambitious and rewarding. The stakes are high, and Kant offers an original and penetrating vision, which has reorientated philosophy ever since. In a mere 18 pages, he attempts to bring together reason, freedom, autonomy, morality, obligation, and his own complex philosophical system of transcendental idealism, in an attempt to vindicate the supreme principle of morality.

As we have seen, in Sections I and II, Kant identifies and analyses the supreme principle of morality. A large question remains open, however: whether this applies *to us*. And here, Kant deals with three interconnected issues. The first concerns how we could be motivated to act morally, when any *interest* we might take in doing so would appear to be based on desires or drives, and therefore fall short of acting for the sake of the moral law, and thus of being truly moral. The second issue concerns whether we are even capable of acting independently of our desires driving us, that is, whether or not we are *free*. If we are not free, then morality (as Kant has analysed it in Sections I and II) will be a mere phantasm for us. And the third issue concerns how a categorical *imperative* is possible, namely how morality applies to us in an imperatival form, *requiring* us to act independently of our desires and drives.

Kant attempts all of this—and more—in five short subsections. The most helpful way to follow Kant's argument is to take these issues one by one, using Kant's own headings.

THE CONCEPT OF FREEDOM IS THE KEY TO EXPLAINING THE AUTONOMY OF THE WILL

Kant begins with a definition of a free will, which involves the capability to initiate action independently of determination by any alien causes (4:446), that is, to determine one's own will. He notes that this is a *negative* characterization of freedom, but that a richer *positive* concept 'flows' from it, in the following way.

Kant thinks of the will as a kind of causality. He claims that causality involves laws, and that a free will thus also involves laws. We then face the question of what kind of laws these will be. Kant claims that natural laws will not suffice, as natural necessity is *heteronomous* because here everything is determined by *something else*. He then asks: 'What else, then, can freedom of the will be, other than autonomy—that is, the property the will has of being a law to itself?' (4:446–7). This is a breathtakingly ambitious but simple argument. Kant claims that heteronomy involves being determined *by something else*, and thus freedom of the will has to involve *being a law to itself*, namely autonomy.

But Kant is not yet done. Having attempted to connect freedom to autonomy, in the very same paragraph he now looks to connect autonomy to morality. He claims that the will being autonomous or a law to itself is the same as it acting only on those maxims which can be willed as universal laws, that is, the FUL or supreme principle of morality. He thus concludes that 'a free will and a will under moral laws are one and the same' (4:447).

Kant thinks that this shows that morality follows from mere *analysis* of the concept of freedom. The basic idea seems to be that being perfectly free just means following the FUL and thus the moral law (as Kant takes himself to have shown that freedom, autonomy, and morality are analytically connected).

Then, in one of the more puzzling parts of Section III, Kant claims that there is also a *synthetic* proposition in the offing. Although it is not even clear what that proposition is (see our explanatory note), what bringing in a synthetic proposition allows Kant to do is to introduce the thought that the connection between a good will and FUL involves a 'third thing', as some such 'third thing' is always required to connect the two parts of a synthetic proposition, since the predicate cannot simply be analysed out of the subject. Cryptically here, Kant says the 'third thing' is 'supplied by' and 'pointed to' by positive freedom, though he cannot at this juncture tell us further what it is—but this 'third thing' will play a key role in solving the three problems outlined earlier. However, before we see what this 'third thing' is, and how it provides such a solution, Kant tells us that we need to do some further preparatory work, which he begins by discussing freedom.

FREEDOM MUST BE PRESUPPOSED AS A PROPERTY OF THE WILL OF ALL RATIONAL BEINGS

For Kant, morality applies to all rational beings. Given this, it is not enough just to show that we human beings are free; Kant also wants to establish a connection between freedom and *all* rational beings. He attempts this by making two bold claims, again, all in one paragraph. The first is that 'every being who cannot act except *under the idea of freedom*, is precisely because of that free in a practical respect; that is, all laws that are inseparably bound up with freedom hold for it' (4:448). The second is the claim that every rational being with a will must act under the idea of freedom. With these two claims, Kant hopes to have established a connection between freedom and all rational beings.

While he just states the first claim, Kant has a condensed but powerful argument for the second. He argues that 'it is impossible to think of a reason that would self-consciously receive guidance from elsewhere with regard to its judgements' (4:448), for otherwise 'the subject would then not attribute the determination of judgement to their reason, but to an impulse' (4:448). In other words, Kant holds that part of being rational involves taking one's reason as the author of one's maxims, and thus regarding oneself as free insofar as one is a rational being. Through this, he looks to establish that we have to think of our judgements as involving this kind of activity, and more broadly, of reason as involving freedom.

OF THE INTEREST THAT ATTACHES TO MORALITY

In two pages, Kant has tried to connect: (1) freedom with autonomy and morality; and (2) freedom with being rational. If these connections applied to us, it would show that as rational beings, we are free and therefore that the moral law is not a phantasm for us. But at the beginning of this third subsection, Kant does not draw this conclusion. Instead he stops to wonder whether we *are* rational beings with wills in the first place, and so whether this argument does apply to us at all.

He also returns to the issue discussed in Sections I and II, namely, how is it that we take an *interest* in the moral law, independently of any desires driving us? In response, he remarks that independently of our desires we can have an interest in being worthy of being happy, but this assumes that the moral law has value for us. The question then is why we see such incomparable value in following the moral law, such that we are prepared to sacrifice all of our empirical happiness for it.

Kant then notes that 'a kind of circle appears here' (4:450). This is a notoriously unclear claim, but one reading is as follows. The difficulty that worries Kant is that his response to the question he has just raised is *circular*, in that we take ourselves to be free in order to put ourselves under the moral law and so claim a moral worth that is said to have incomparable value; but we put ourselves under the moral law only because we take ourselves to be free. However, this is merely to go back and forth as if it were clear why we should place value on following the moral law and freedom in the first place, and not to explain why we should.

Thankfully, Kant thinks, there is a way out of this circle. For this, he introduces *transcendental idealism* for the first time in the *Groundwork*. 'Transcendental idealism' is the name of the grand philosophical system, which he put forward in the *Critique of Pure Reason* four years earlier, in 1781.

Kant introduces transcendental idealism in the *Groundwork* with the following claim: 'all representations that come to us involuntarily (like those of the senses) enable us to know objects as they affect us,

while what they may be in themselves remains unknown to us' (4:451).
He thus claims that 'we can only achieve knowledge of *appearances*,
never of *things in themselves*' (4:451). Kant is eager to insist that this
can be easily understood; indeed, he even claims that this point
'requires no subtle thinking, and . . . one can assume even the commonest understanding can grasp [it]' (4:450). So what is the basic
claim? Transcendental idealism is the position that *appearances* are
not *things in themselves*. In the *Critique of Pure Reason*, Kant argues
that how things *appear* to us in our experience is not the way things
are *in themselves*, as appearances are formed by the fundamental
structures through which we shape experience (such as space and
time, and categories like substance and cause), whereas things-in-
themselves are not. Kant thinks that this gives rise to a further distinction between two worlds: the world of sense (appearances) and
the world of understanding (things in themselves).

And now comes the crucial move. Kant thinks that we belong to
both worlds. He writes that 'with respect to mere perception and
receptivity to sensations the subject must count themselves as belonging to the *world of sense*' (4:451). In addition though, 'as regards what
there may be of pure activity in them (that which reaches consciousness, not by affecting the sense, but immediately), the subject must
count themselves as belonging to the *intellectual world* [or world of
understanding]' (4:451).

Kant continues by claiming that *reason* also reveals in us a capacity
which distinguishes us from all other things in the empirical world.
Reason's capacity to generate—what Kant calls—*ideas*, that is concepts (such as God or the soul) that go beyond anything afforded to us
by the world of sense, 'shows a spontaneity so pure' that it reveals our
membership in the 'world of understanding' (4:452). Our capacity for
reason therefore shows that we are members of the world of understanding (or intellectual world), where we are free from all natural laws
and thus of the determining causes which govern the world of sense.

This appeal to transcendental idealism therefore provides us with
reasons to think we are free in a way which removes the previous threat
of a circle. In doing so, Kant has provided an answer to the question of
how it is that we can act independently of our desires and drives. In the
next subsection, he goes on to show how transcendental idealism also

addresses the other two issues of how a categorical *imperative* is possible and how it is that we can take an *interest* in morality.

HOW IS A CATEGORICAL IMPERATIVE POSSIBLE?

Kant now turns to consider how it is that, for us, morality takes the form of a categorical imperative. The answer also hinges upon transcendental idealism and our membership in the two worlds.

Kant writes that: 'If I were solely a member of the world of understanding, all my actions would therefore conform perfectly with the autonomy of the pure will' (4:453), which echoes what he has said previously about the holy will. Likewise, he writes that: 'if I were solely an item in the world of sense, [my actions] would have to be taken to conform perfectly with the natural law of desires and inclinations, and hence with the heteronomy of nature' (4:453). If we were only members of the intelligible world, we would not experience morality as an imperative, as we would merely follow the moral law without any resistance from sensible desires. If we were only members of the sensible world, we would lack freedom and the moral law would be a phantasm for us. However, as members of *both* worlds, we have sensible desires, but also the freedom to recognize and follow the moral law independently of them. And this dual constitution of ours means that we experience the moral law as an *imperative*, as it pulls against our sensible desires.

In addition, Kant tells us that the moral law is immediately lawgiving for us because the world of the understanding '*contains the ground*' (4:453) of the world of sense. Here, he seems to be arguing that the world of understanding has some sort of *priority* over the world of sense, which explains why its laws trump the laws of the world of sense for us; indeed later Kant will say that '*what belongs to mere appearance is necessarily subordinated by reason to the way things are in themselves*' (4:461). Kant contends that common human reason confirms this, using the example of 'the most wicked villain', who (Kant claims) when presented with examples of moral behaviour, wishes that they too were so disposed (4:454). But, 'because of their inclinations and impulses they find this hard to bring about in themselves' (4:454) and 'as a result, they wish to be free of such inclinations, which they themselves find burdensome' (4:454). Through this, Kant claims, 'they prove that with a will free from impulses of sensibility, they transfer themselves in thought into an order of things altogether different from that of their desires in the field of sensibility' (4:454).

How exactly this all fits together is a matter of much discussion, but in this section Kant appears to answer the question of how we take the kind of *interest* we do in morality, such that we are prepared to sacrifice all in its name. His answer seems to be that morality, and moral worth, has an incomparable value which even the villain can see, which therefore puts us in an entirely different order from anything to do with the satisfaction of our desires and drives. Kant will return to this issue in the following subsection, where he comments that 'the law interests us because it is valid for us as human beings, since it originates from our will as an intelligence, hence from our actual self' (4:461). This distinction between moral worth and the satisfaction of desires and drives also perhaps relates to the distinction which he drew earlier in the *Groundwork* between dignity and mere price (cf. 4:434): the value of autonomy and being under moral laws simply cannot be compared to empirical satisfaction. It is incomparably higher.

OF THE OUTERMOST BOUNDARY OF ALL PRACTICAL PHILOSOPHY

Not content with connecting reason, freedom, autonomy, morality, obligation, and transcendental idealism, Kant now turns to the 'outermost boundary' of all practical philosophy. In this section he addresses the seeming conflict between free will and determinism (what modern-day philosophers call 'the free will problem'), as well as the limits of human knowledge.

Why does Kant turn to this? He identifies a troubling conflict in reason itself, where *theoretical* reason needs the concept of natural necessity, but *practical* reason needs the concept of freedom (4:455). We have already seen why practical reason needs the concept of freedom, but in the *Critique of Pure Reason*, Kant also argued that the world of experience has to be structured into an order of deterministic causes. Kant claims that speculative philosophy must solve this seeming conflict, for otherwise, we would have to give up the thought of freedom, and in turn morality (4:456).

Transcendental idealism once more turns out to be the key here. The world of appearance is determined by natural necessity, whereas the world of the understanding is not. This allows for natural necessity and freedom to both be valid, each in their own domain. As Kant claims, 'there is not the slightest contradiction in *a thing in appearance* (belonging to the world of sense) being subject to certain laws from which, *as a thing* or being *in itself*, it is independent' (4:457). Transcendental idealism thus removes the seeming conflict between natural necessity and freedom.

Of course, one might wonder how exactly this is supposed to work. One might naturally want to know more about the world of understanding. What is it like? And what objects does it contain? How do they affect our will? However, Kant thinks that these issues are beyond our grasp—hence the reference to the 'outermost boundary' of practical philosophy. With transcendental idealism, Kant hopes to avoid what he sees as the dogmatic metaphysics of rationalist thinkers, who make what Kant regards as all sorts of ungrounded assertions about things beyond the empirical world and knowledge, such as God, ultimate reality, and human freedom. Kant insists that *our* knowledge is confined to the world of appearance, and here, this means that while he insists we rightly take an interest in morality, have freedom, and are practically rational, he cannot explain the mechanisms that make these things possible (4:459–60), as our only way of grasping such a mechanism is in causal terms which only apply to the world of sense, not the world of the understanding. Indeed, Kant even suggests that it is a good thing that we cannot understand these topics in these terms, for if the interest we take in morality could be explained in these ways then 'there would be no morality' (4:463). Kant thus ends the *Groundwork* by claiming that 'although we do not comprehend the unconditional practical necessity of the moral imperative, we do comprehend its incomprehensibility' (4:463), insofar as transcendental idealism helps us understand the bounds of our cognitive powers, even though of course it cannot help us overstep them.

What Should We Make of Kant's Ethics? A Brief Overview and Assessment

So far we have concentrated on providing an understanding of Kant's line of argument and the structure of the text. Now we turn to consider what we should make of Kant's claims.

As we have seen, Kant's project in the *Groundwork* is to identify and vindicate the supreme principle of morality. And as we said at the outset, this project involves the following broad areas: the *content*, *authority* and *reality* of morality, and the relation between morality and human *nature* or human *capacities*. We can now summarize the position Kant takes on these questions, and consider how we should evaluate his view.

With regard to the *content* of morality, Kant's concern with duty, imperatives and the moral law means that he is usually classified as a deontologist, that is, someone who thinks that morality forbids or requires certain actions (while leaving many other actions simply permitted). Indeed, his view is often taken to be the foremost example of an alternative to a Divine Command deontology—that is, a view on which actions are forbidden or required by God. On a deontological view, what makes an action right is not whether it has good consequences for human life (as on utilitarianism), or whether it exhibits virtues such as courage or benevolence or friendship (as on an Aristotelian virtue ethics), but rather its conformity to what is morally required. As we have seen, on Kant's view the basic form of the moral law is that one must never act in a way that cannot be universalized; this principle is also articulated as the (purportedly equivalent) requirement that one must never treat a human being as a mere means to an end.

Kant gives us examples to illustrate these principles, ruling out lying promises, suicide, failures to help those in need, and failures to develop one's own talents. However, these examples have proven highly controversial, and a question worth raising is whether his account of the basic principle stands or falls with these examples. One challenge is that Kant's view of basic wrongs as those where a person treats another as a mere means seems best to fit cases like coercion, deception, and manipulation, in which one person uses another by in some way subverting or bypassing that person's reasoning capacities and therefore treating them merely as a source of opportunity rather than a being with value in their own right. Resonant though Kant's view is as an explanation of what is wrong with *some* things that human beings might wrongfully do to one another, it nevertheless appears to neglect other important evils such as murder, violence, or inflicting pointless, intense suffering that are aimed at our bodily rather than our rational nature.

Another challenge is that the centrality Kant's view gives to rational agency seems to leave Kant's view unable to account for duties to non-rational beings, including animals, human infants, and those suffering from dementia. And a further issue is that there seem to be exceptions to the wrongness of e.g. a lying promise, whereas presumably the basic principle that Kant has identified must be exceptionless— if it were not, then there would have to be a yet more fundamental principle explaining when the exceptions are justified and why. While debates continue over what Kant is, and should be, committed to on each of these questions, there are clearly some challenges that would need to be overcome in order to make his view convincing. Nevertheless, the idea that at least some wrongs consist in the *objectification* of human beings—treating them as things, or as mere means, as the Formula of Humanity puts it—has become central to debates in feminism and elsewhere.

In regard to the issue of the *authority* of morality, Kant's view has split opinion. First of all, there are those who agree with Kant's own assessment that his idea of morality as a categorical imperative, binding those subject to it unconditionally and regardless of any prior motivation that they might have, is an undeniable insight that any adequate account of morality has to recognize. After all, this camp might say, how can the wrongness of, say, inflicting intense pain on an innocent person in any way be affected by whether this is the kind of thing we have motivations either towards or against? Of course, the feelings of the person *subjected* to the pain are important—but how can the feelings of the agent *doing* the inflicting, such as whether they take pleasure in it, or happen to feel emotions of shame or guilt, be in any way relevant to whether it is wrong? For this camp it is a corruption of morality to start to look for non-moral motivations that moral conduct might appeal to—it is essential to right thinking about morality, on this view, that it should be seen as its own reason, its force independent of any of our other desires, drives, or emotions.

However, there have been doubters. Some have argued that, whatever morality is, it must be made for human beings, and as well as taking our physical and psychological welfare into account in determining the content of morality, we should also be guided by empirically exist-ing human capacities in determining how much morality can demand of us. David Hume is often taken as the standard-bearer for this tradition, arguing that morality is rooted in naturally occurring pas-sions, and that no set of standards could have authority over us that does not go through those passions. Moral standards may appear to us as external and imposing, but in reality, Humeans say, this appear-ance is a result of our unknowingly projecting our own feelings on to the situations that cause them.

Whether a categorical imperative is possible might be said to depend on the remaining two issues: whether our best understanding of reality has a place for the existence of unconditionally binding moral standards, or whether like witchcraft it is a belief in the reality of which the progress of science will gradually deprive us; and whether, even if indeed there are such standards, human beings have the *capacities* to recognize and respond to them. Kant raises the question whether a categorical imperative is possible, and clearly thinks he has a positive answer to it, but as we have made clear earlier, it is far from obvious exactly what that answer amounts to.

In regard to the reality of moral standards, Kant might be inter-preted as holding that there is one thing, and one thing only, that has intrinsic value, and which is therefore a source of awe and reverence to us: this thing he thinks of variously as the moral law, the good will, autonomy, or simply reason. These terms might be thought of as ultimately referring to the same thing: rational agency, or the con-formity of agency with rational standards. On this 'intrinsic value' interpretation, rational agency has value incomparable to anything else in the world: unlike anything else, Kant thinks, it has dignity beyond all price. This would be to interpret Kant as a moral realist, one who holds that among all the properties that objects in the world might have, there is a property possessed by some objects that marks them out as requiring special treatment (indeed reverence), and which is the property of dignity.

However, there are many philosophers who are convinced that moral realism is an untenable position, that science reveals to us a basically materialist world that has no place for essentially prescriptive proper-ties such as dignity. These philosophers think instead that Kant has offered us a way of preserving the authority of morality while reject-ing moral realism. They think that Kant's emphasis on the connec-tion between morality and rationality shows that an unconditionally binding set of moral standards can be constructed from uncondition-ally binding rational standards. Just as it is point blank irrational to have two inconsistent beliefs, so, they would say, it is point blank irrational to act in such a way as to defeat one's own ends (indeed, this is the point of the authority of hypothetical imperatives). Yet the irrationality of self-defeating action does not depend, on this line, on properties existing in reality. Rather it is internal to the demands of action itself, since action aims at some purpose, and thus to fail to further that purpose would be to fail properly to act. There therefore seems to be a kind of necessity, on this approach, to the demand that we not act in such a way as to defeat our own ends—though of course not a necessity that we necessarily comply with. These 'constructiv-ist' philosophers argue that moral standards have the authority of practical reason—that as well as telling us not to defeat our ends (hypothetical imperatives), practical reason tells us not to act in ways that cannot be universalized (the categorical imperative) and that this does not require us to believe, as on the realist view, in any essen-tially prescriptive properties. Whatever the result of this debate between realist and constructivist interpretations of Kant, it is clear that both stand in opposition to any Humean view that sees moral standards as a result of the contingencies of natural human passions.

One thing that interpreters of Kant have to agree on, therefore, is that—to turn to our final issue—Kant has a strongly rationalistic picture of human agency. The centrepiece of his theory is rational agency. This is not to say, of course, that Kant thinks that we always, or even often, behave rationally. However, he clearly thinks that we have it within us to raise ourselves above the influence of our natural and social inheritance, and act autonomously—by which he means, acting on the basis of our recognition of the rational force of a demand, rather than its appeal to any aspect of our psychology, such as our pride, our desire, our fear, and so on. This aspect of Kant has proven deeply enduring. The idea that human action and behaviour must be explained in terms that are ultimately discontinuous with the explanations that we can give to natural phenomena—that, for instance, human decisions cannot in the end be seen as the result of instincts, automatic responses to stimuli, or impersonal social forces—is a live position in the philosophies of psychology and social action. While research programmes in these subjects often seem to proceed on the assumption that a fully deterministic explanation will be discovered if only there is enough time to do so, a powerful position remains that insists, in a Kantian spirit, that attempting to explain human behaviour without reference to the influence of rational standards will always end in failure.

However, does Kant have any good argument in the *Groundwork* for the claim that we are indeed sufficiently free of determination by psychological or social forces to be able to think for ourselves, recognize the independent force of rational requirements, and conform our action to them? The most he seems to offer us is the perhaps baffling possibility that transcendental idealism holds out, of our membership of two worlds. However, what has been most enduring in these cryptic remarks is effectively the position outlined in the preceding paragraph, that explanations of human behaviour cannot be exhausted by what is available to the scientific perspective, that rational standards have force for us, and hence that we act under the idea of freedom.

NOTE ON THE TRANSLATION
AND THE TEXT

THE *Groundwork* has not lacked for translators, particularly in recent years, and now some nine versions in English are available (see the Select Bibliography for details), most of which have been consulted in preparing this version. Unlike many of these, our aim (in keeping with the ethos of the Oxford World's Classics series as a whole) has been to target our translation at the 'general reader' rather than the specialist or scholar, so that we have felt able to be freer with the text than some versions, while still aiming to be accurate. As well as detracting from the readability of Kant's text, following the original too literally can also obscure his meaning. German academic prose can be notorious for its complexity and heaviness, and Kant is notorious for being a German academic par excellence; thus, his often-already complex and subtle ideas and arguments can be very hard for the reader to follow and understand, much less enjoy. In order to break down some of these barriers, and to make his work a little more accessible to a contemporary audience, we have therefore felt justified in departing from other more literal translations in various ways.

One significant change is that we have often broken up and restructured Kant's famously long sentences, and on occasions also his long paragraphs, which can be especially trying to the English-speaking reader. In some places, we have also added some signposting and italicization, to help the reader better follow the flow of Kant's argument.

More controversially, perhaps, we have allowed ourselves some flexibility in the translation of some German words, taking context into account, except in cases where we think it is important for the reader to follow that the same German word is being used or repeated. We have also tried to use more common English words where possible, rather than rather technical philosophical terms (such as 'knowledge' rather than 'cognition' for *Erkenntnis*). Where possible we have also translated Kant's use of Latin terms directly into English, and have used gender neutral language.

Kant's own notes are reproduced as footnotes and are marked by roman numerals. Our notes are marked by an asterisk, and are to be found after the translation, keyed to the relevant page number of this edition.

This translation is based on the new edition of the German text to be found in Gregor and Timmermann's German–English edition of the *Groundwork* (again see the Select Bibliography). This follows the second edition which was published in Riga by Johann Friedrich Hartknoch in 1786, after Kant made some minor corrections and changes to the first edition of 1785, with some further minor emendations by Timmermann. As is now customary in Kant translations, we have added in the margins a reference to the pagination of the text found in the Akademie edition of Kant's works, where the *Groundwork* is published in volume 4, which is therefore combined with these page numbers as the standard way to refer to his writings—e.g. 4:394.

We would also like to express our deep gratitude for the help given to us by the following readers (though of course any remaining errors are our own): Stephen Bennett, Michael Perraudin, David Strohmaier, and Martin Sticker.

SELECT BIBLIOGRAPHY

Collected works of Kant

Kant's gesammelte Schriften, ed. the Royal Prussian (later German, then Berlin-Brandenburg) Academy of Sciences. 29 vols. Berlin: Georg Reimer (later Walter de Gruyter), 1900–.

The Cambridge Edition of the Works of Immanuel Kant, ed. Paul Guyer and Allen W. Wood, 15 vols. Cambridge, UK: Cambridge University Press, 1997–.

Translations of Kant's Groundwork

Abbott, Thomas K., rev. Lara Denis (trans.), Groundwork for the Metaphysics of Morals. Peterborough, Ontario: Broadview Press, 2005.

Beck, Lewis White (trans.), Foundations of the Metaphysics of Morals, 2nd edn. Upper Saddle River, NJ: Prentice Hall, 1997.

Ellington, James W. (trans.), Grounding for the Metaphysics of Morals, 2nd edn. Indianapolis: Hackett, 1981.

Gregor, Mary (trans.), Groundwork of the Metaphysics of Morals, in Kant's Practical Philosophy, trans. and ed. Mary Gregory, in The Cambridge Edition of the Works of Immanuel Kant, 41–108. Cambridge, UK: Cambridge University Press, 1996

Gregor, Mary, and Jens Timmermann (trans.), Groundwork of the Metaphysics, a German–English edition. Cambridge, UK: Cambridge University Press, 2011.

Gregor, Mary, and Jens Timmermann (trans.), Groundwork of the Metaphysics of Morals, rev. edn. Cambridge, UK: Cambridge University Press, 2012.

Paton, H. J. (trans.), The Moral Law. London: Hutchinson, 1948. Retitled as Groundwork of the Metaphysics of Morals. New York: Harper & Row, 1964.

Wood, Allen W. (trans.), Groundwork for the Metaphysics of Morals. New Haven, CT, and London: Yale University Press, 2002.

Zweig, Arnulf (trans.), Groundwork for the Metaphysics of Morals. Oxford: Oxford University Press, 2002.

General discussions of Kant's life and thought

Ameriks, Karl, Interpreting Kant's Critiques. Oxford: Oxford University Press, 2003.

Cassirer, Ernst, Kant's Life and Work. New Haven, CT: Yale University Press, 1981.

Guyer, Paul, *Kant*. London: Routledge, 2006.
Guyer, Paul (ed.), *The Cambridge Companion to Kant*. Cambridge, UK: Cambridge University Press, 1992.
Guyer, Paul (ed.), *The Cambridge Companion to Kant and Modern Philosophy*. Cambridge, UK: Cambridge University Press, 2006.
Kuehn, Manfred, *Kant: A Biography*. Cambridge, UK: Cambridge University Press, 2001.
Ward, Anthony, *Kant: The Three Critiques*. Cambridge, UK: Polity, 2006.

Introductory works on Kant's Groundwork

Acton, H. B., *Kant's Moral Philosophy*. London: Macmillan, 1970.
Hill, Thomas E. Jr., 'Editor's Introduction: Some Main Themes of the *Groundwork* and Analysis of the Argument', in Arnulf Zweig (trans.), *Groundwork for the Metaphysics of Morals*, 19–178. Oxford: Oxford University Press, 2002.
Korsgaard, Christine M., 'Introduction', in Mary Gregor and Jens Timmermann (trans.), *Groundwork of the Metaphysics of Morals*, rev. edn, ix–xxxvi. Cambridge, UK: Cambridge University Press, 2012.
Paton, H. J., 'Analysis of the Argument', in H. J. Paton (trans.), *The Moral Law*, 13–52. London: Hutchinson, 1948.
Sullivan, Roger J., *An Introduction to Kant's Ethics*. Cambridge, UK: Cambridge University Press, 1994.
Uleman, Jennifer, *An Introduction to Kant's Moral Philosophy*. Cambridge, UK: Cambridge University Press, 2010.
Velleman, David, 'Reading Kant's *Groundwork*', in George Sher (ed.), *Ethics: Essential Readings in Moral Theory*, 343–59. London: Routledge, 2012.
Wood, Allen W., *Formulas of the Moral Law*. Cambridge, UK: Cambridge University Press, 2017).

Commentaries on Kant's Groundwork

Allison, Henry, *Kant's 'Groundwork for the Metaphysics of Morals'*. Oxford: Oxford University Press, 2011.
Cholbi, Michael, *Understanding Kant's Ethics*. Cambridge, UK: Cambridge University Press, 2016.
Guyer, Paul, *Kant's 'Groundwork for the Metaphysics of Morals'*. London: Continuum, 2007.
Paton, H. J., *The Categorical Imperative: A Study in Kant's Philosophy*. London: Hutchinson, 1947.
Ross, David, *Kant's Ethical Theory*. Oxford: Oxford University Press, 1954.

Schönecker, Dieter, and Allen W. Wood (2015), *Immanuel Kant's 'Groundwork for the Metaphysics of Morals'*. Cambridge, MA: Harvard University Press, 2015.

Sedgwick, Sally, *Kant's 'Groundwork of the Metaphysics of Morals'*. Cambridge, UK: Cambridge University Press, 2008.

Timmermann, Jens, *Kant's 'Groundwork of the Metaphysics of Morals': A Commentary*. Cambridge, UK: Cambridge University Press, 2007.

Wolff, Robert P., *The Autonomy of Reason: A Commentary on Kant's 'Groundwork of the Metaphysic of Morals'*. Gloucester, MA: Peter Smith, 1986.

Works on Kant's Groundwork *and his ethics more generally*

Allison, Henry, *Kant's Theory of Freedom*. Cambridge, UK: Cambridge University Press, 1990.

Aune, Bruce, *Kant's Theory of Morals*. Princeton, NJ: Princeton University Press, 1979.

Baron, Marcia, *Kantian Ethics (Almost) Without Apology*. Ithaca, NY: Cornell University Press, 1995.

Dean, Richard, *The Value of Humanity in Kant's Moral Theory*. Cambridge, UK: Cambridge University Press, 2006.

Grenberg, Jeanine, *Kant's Defense of Common Moral Experience*. Cambridge, UK: Cambridge University Press, 2013.

Guyer, Paul, *Kant on Freedom, Law and Happiness*. Cambridge, UK: Cambridge University Press, 2000.

Guyer, Paul (ed.), *Groundwork of the Metaphysics of Morals: Critical Essays*. Lanham, MD: Rowman and Littlefield, 1998.

Herman, Barbara, *The Practice of Moral Judgment*. Cambridge, MA: Harvard University Press, 1993.

Hill, Thomas E. Jr., *Dignity and Practical Reason in Kant's Moral Theory*. Ithaca, NY: Cornell University Press, 1992.

Hill, Thomas E. Jr. (ed.), *The Blackwell Guide to Kant's Ethics*. Oxford: Wiley-Blackwell, 2009.

Kerstein, Samuel, *Kant's Search for the Supreme Principle of Morality*. Cambridge, UK: Cambridge University Press, 2002.

Korsgaard, Christine M., *Creating the Kingdom of Ends*. Cambridge, UK: Cambridge University Press, 1996.

O'Neill, Onora, *Acting on Principle: An Essay on Kantian Ethics*, 2nd edn. Cambridge, UK: Cambridge University Press, 2013.

O'Neill, Onora, *Constructions of Reason: Explorations of Kant's Practical Philosophy*. Cambridge, UK: Cambridge University Press, 1989.

Rawls, John, *Lectures on the History of Moral Philosophy*, 143–325. Cambridge, MA: Harvard University Press, 2000.

Reath, Andrews, *Agency and Autonomy in Kant's Moral Theory*. Oxford: Oxford University Press, 2006.

Stern, Robert, *Kantian Ethics: Value, Agency, and Obligation*. Oxford: Oxford University Press, 2015.

Stratton-Lake, Philip, *Kant, Duty, and Moral Worth*. London: Routledge, 2000.

Timmermann, Jens (ed.), *Kant's 'Groundwork of the Metaphysics of Morals': A Critical Guide*. Cambridge, UK: Cambridge University Press, 2009.

Wood, Allen W., *Kantian Ethics*. Cambridge, UK: Cambridge University Press, 2008.

Wood, Allen W., *Kant's Ethical Thought*. Cambridge, UK: Cambridge University Press, 1999.

A CHRONOLOGY OF IMMANUEL KANT

1724 Born on 22 April in
Königsberg, East Prussia (now
Kaliningrad, Russia)

1730–2 Attends elementary school at
Vorstädter Hospitalschule

1732–40 Attends the pietistic *Collegium
Fridericianum*

1737 Death of Kant's mother

1740   Death of Frederick William I and
                                                  accession of Frederick II ('Frederick the
                                                  Great')

1740–6 Enrols at the University of
Königsberg and studies
mathematics, natural science, and
theology, leaving without a degree

1746 Death of Kant's father

1747–54 Employed as a private tutor for
families in the Königsberg area

1749 Publishes *Thoughts on the*   Birth of Goethe
Estimation of Living Forces
(written 1744–6)

1754 Returns to Königsberg   Death of Wolff

1755 Publishes *Universal Natural
History and Theory of the
Heavens*; promotion to
magister with thesis 'Concise
Outline of Some Reflections
on Fire'; acquires permission
to lecture as *Privatdozent* at
university with thesis 'A New
Exposition of the First
Principles of Metaphysics'

1756 Publishes three essays on the
Lisbon earthquake; the
doctoral dissertation *Physical
Monadology*; and 'New
Observations on the Theory of
the Winds'

Unsuccessfully applies for
a professorship in logic and
metaphysics at the University
of Königsberg

1759   Birth of Schiller

1762 Publishes 'The False Subtlety   Rousseau publishes *Émile* and *The Social*
      of the Four Syllogistic Figures'   *Contract*; birth of Fichte

      Herder becomes Kant's
      student (until 1764)

1763 Publishes *The Only Possible*
      Basis for a Demonstration of the
      Existence of God and 'An
      Attempt to Introduce the
      Concept of Negative
      Quantities into Philosophy'

1764 Declines offer of Professorship
      of Poetry

      Publishes *Observations on the*
      Feeling of the Beautiful and the
      Sublime and the second-prize
      essay for the Berlin Academy
      Enquiry Concerning the
      Distinctness of the Principles of
      Natural Theology and Morals

1765   Posthumous publication of Leibniz's
                                           New Essays on the Human
                                           Understanding

1766 Publishes*Dreamsofa Spirit-Seer*
      ElucidatedbyDreamsofMetaphysics

      Begins correspondence with
      Mendelssohn

1768 Publishes 'On the Ultimate
      Ground of the Differences of
      Direction in Space'

1769 Declines offer of professorship
      in Erlangen

1770 Declines offer of professorship   Birth of Hegel
      in Jena; appointed Professor of
      Logic and Metaphysics in
      Königsberg

	Publishes the inaugural dissertation *On the Forms and Principles of the Sensible and the Intelligible World*	
1770–80	The so-called 'silent decade' during which Kant works on his new 'critical' project	
1772	Letter to Marcus Herz on 21 February outlining project of *Critique of Pure Reason*	
1775	Publishes 'On the Difference of Human Races' as announcement for anthropology lectures	Birth of Schelling
1776	Becomes Dean of the Faculty of Philosophy for first time (serves eight times)	Death of Hume; the American 'Declaration of Independence' and the 'Declaration of the Rights of Man'
1778	Declines offer of professorship in Halle	Deaths of Rousseau and Voltaire
1781	Publishes the *Critique of Pure Reason*	Death of Lessing
1783	Publishes *Prolegomena to Any Future Metaphysics*	
1784	Publishes 'Idea for a Universal History from a Cosmopolitan Point of View' and 'An Answer to the Question: What is Enlightenment?'	
1785	Publishes *Groundwork for the Metaphysics of Morals*	
1786	Publishes the second edition of the *Groundwork*; *The Metaphysical Foundations of Natural Science*; 'The Conjectural Beginning of Human History'; and 'What Does "Orientation in Thinking" Mean?'	Death of Frederick the Great and accession of Frederick William II; death of Mendelssohn
	Elected Rector of the University of Königsberg and becomes external member of the Berlin Academy of Sciences	

1786–7		Reinhold publishes his *Letters on the Kantian Philosophy*
1787	Second edition of the *Critique of Pure Reason*	
1788	Publishes the *Critique of Practical Reason*	Death of Hamann
1789		Beginning of French Revolution
1790	Publishes the *Critique of Judgement*, and polemic against Eberhard: 'On a Discovery That is to Make All New Critique of Pure Reason Dispensable Because of an Older One'	Maimon publishes *Essay on Transcendental Philosophy*
1791	Publishes 'On the Failure of All Attempts at Theodicy'	
1792	Publishes essay which will become Part I of *Religion within the Limits of Reason Alone*	France declared a republic, and execution of Louis XIV
	Fichte's *Essay towards a Critique of All Revelation* appears anonymously and is widely attributed to Kant	
1793	Publishes whole of *Religion within the Limits of Reason Alone* and 'On the Common Saying: That may be Right in Theory but is not Valid in Practice'; second edition of the *Critique of Judgement*	Schiller publishes *On Grace and Dignity*
1794	Elected member of the St Petersburg Academy of Sciences; comes into conflict with the Prussian Censor and receives royal reprimand for publishing *Religion within the Limits of Reason*	Fichte publishes *Grounding of the Entire Doctrine of Science (Wissenschaftslehre)*
		Robespierre guillotined
1795	Publishes *Toward Perpetual Peace*	Schiller publishes *Letters on the Aesthetic Education of Man*
		Schelling publishes *On the Ego as the Principle of Philosophy*

1796	Publishes 'On a Newly Elevated Tone in Philosophy'	Fichte publishes *Foundations of Natural Law*
	Gives his final lecture at the University of Köningsberg	
1797	Publishes *The Metaphysics of Morals* and 'On a Presumed Right to Lie from Philanthropic Motives'	Death of Frederick William II, accession of Frederick William III
		Schelling publishes *Ideas for a Philosophy of Nature*
1798	Publishes *The Conflict of the Faculties* and *Anthropology from a Pragmatic Point of View*	Schelling publishes *Of the Worldsoul*
1799	Publishes 'Open Declaration against Fichte'	Herder publishes *Metacritique*
	Third edition of the *Critique of Judgement*	
1800	Publication of Kant's *Logic*, edited by Jäsche	Schelling publishes *System of Transcendental Idealism*
1801		Schiller publishes 'On the Sublime'
		Hegel publishes *The Difference between Fichte's and Schelling's Systems of Philosophy*
1802	Publication of Kant's *Physical Geography*, edited by Rink	Schelling and Hegel edit the *Critical Journal of Philosophy*, and Hegel publishes *Faith and Knowledge* in the journal
1803	Publication of Kant's *Pedagogy*, edited by Rink	
1804	Death of Kant on 12 February, buried on 28 February	
	Publication of the prize essay *On the Progress of Metaphysics since Leibniz and Wolff*, edited by Rink (written in 1790)	Napoleon crowned Emperor of France
1900	Academy edition of Kant's writings inaugurated by Dilthey	
1936–8	Publication of Kant's *Opus postumum* in the Academy edition	

GROUNDWORK FOR THE
METAPHYSICS OF MORALS

ANCIENT Greek philosophy was divided into three disciplines: *physics*, *ethics*, and *logic*. This is perfectly adequate and needs no improvement, except perhaps in this respect: to understand the principle for dividing philosophy in this way, partly to be sure of its completeness, and partly to see how it is to be further subdivided.

All rational knowledge is either *material* and considers some object, or it is *formal*, and concerns itself merely with the form of the understanding and of reason itself, and the universal rules of thinking in general, regardless of what that thinking is about. Formal philosophy is called *logic*; but material philosophy, which has to do with objects and the laws to which they are subject, is once again divided into two. For these laws are either laws of *nature* or of *freedom*. The study of the first is *physics*, of the second *ethics*. The former is also called 'natural philosophy', the latter 'moral philosophy'.

Logic can have no empirical part, that is, no part in which the universal and necessary laws of thought are based on experience; for then it would not be logic, that is, an authoritative set of rules for reason and the understanding, which hold valid for all thought and require demonstration. By contrast, both natural and moral philosophy can have their empirical part, since the former must formulate the laws of nature as we know it through experience, while the latter must formulate the laws for the will of human beings insofar as they are affected by this nature. The first are laws in accordance with which everything happens, while the second are those in accordance with which 388 everything *ought* to happen, but also giving due consideration to the conditions under which what ought to happen often does not happen.

All philosophy which is based on experience can be called *empirical*; but that which is based on a priori principles alone is called *pure*.* The latter, when it is purely formal, is called *logic*; but if it is confined to certain objects of the understanding, it is called *metaphysics*.

In this way metaphysics divides in two: a *metaphysics of nature* and a *metaphysics of morals*. Physics will thus have its empirical but also its rational part, and the same will be true for ethics—but here the

empirical part might be called *practical anthropology*,* and the rational
part properly called *moral theory*.*

All trades, crafts, and arts have gained through the division of
labour, whereby no one does everything, but each limits themselves to
significantly different tasks so that they can then perform them perfectly and with greater ease. Where labour is not divided and shared
out in this way, where each person is a jack-of-all-trades, trades are
still sunk in utter barbarism. One could well ask whether pure philosophy (in all its parts) might not require its own specialist; whether it
would not be better for this whole trade if those who, in accordance
with public taste, are in the habit of peddling parts of the empirical
mixed unawares with the rational—who call themselves 'independent thinkers', and call the others, who deal with the merely rational
part, 'navel gazers'—were warned against carrying on two trades at
once, when they are in fact to be pursued in very different ways, perhaps each requiring a special talent, which when combined in one
person makes only a bungler. But here I confine myself to asking
whether the nature of the inquiry itself requires that the empirical
part should always be carefully separated from the rational one, so
that actual (empirical) physics must be prefaced by a metaphysics of
nature, and practical anthropology must be prefaced by a metaphysics
of morals; and whether these must be carefully cleansed of everything
empirical, in order to know how much pure reason can accomplish in
each case, and what the sources are from which it draws its own teaching a priori, and if this latter business can be pursued by all teachers
of morals (whose name is legion) or only by some, who feel a calling
for it.

Since my focus is moral wisdom, I limit myself to just this question: is it not of the utmost necessity to work out for once a pure
moral philosophy, completely cleansed of everything that might be in
some way empirical and so belong to anthropology? That there must
be such a thing is clear just from the common idea of duty and of
moral laws. Everyone must admit that a law, if it is to hold morally, i.e.
as the ground of an obligation, must do so with absolute necessity;
that the commandment 'thou shalt not lie' does not just hold for
human beings only, as though other rational beings did not have to
heed it; and likewise with all the other genuine moral laws. Hence the

ground of obligation must not be sought in the nature of the human, or in the circumstances of the world in which we are placed, but a priori solely in concepts of pure reason. Any other precept that is founded on principles of mere experience—even one that might in a certain sense be considered universal—can be called a practical rule but never a moral law, to the extent that it rests in the least part on empirical grounds, if only in its motive.

Thus not only do moral laws, along with their principles, differ essentially from all the rest of practical knowledge, in which there is something empirical; rather all moral philosophy rests entirely on its pure part, and applied to human beings, does not borrow in the slightest from the knowledge of them found in anthropology, but gives them laws a priori as rational beings. This of course still requires a power of judgement sharpened by experience, partly to distinguish in what cases they apply, and partly to open up the will to these laws and give them the potency needed for compliance, since human beings are affected by so many inclinations, that while they are indeed capable of the idea of a pure practical reason, they nonetheless cannot so easily make it effective in the concrete reality of their lives.

A metaphysics of morals is thus indispensably necessary, not merely on theoretical grounds—that is, in order to investigate the source 390 of the practical principles that lie a priori in our reason—but also because moral conduct remains exposed to all sorts of corruption as long as we lack that guiding thread and supreme norm for their correct judgement. For in order to be morally good, it is not enough to *conform* to the moral law, but one must act *for its sake*. Otherwise this conformity is only chancy and precarious, since although the non-moral* motivations will now and then produce actions that conform to the law, they will in many cases produce actions that transgress it. However, the moral law in its purity and authenticity (which is what is most important in practical matters) is to be sought nowhere else than in pure philosophy, so this (as metaphysics) must come first, and without it there can be no moral philosophy at all. Indeed a philosophy which mixes together these pure principles with empirical ones does not even deserve the name of philosophy. For philosophy treats as separate what common rational knowledge only grasps as mixed. Still less does it deserve the name of moral philosophy, since by this very mixing it even manages to infringe on the purity of morals themselves and is thereby self-defeating.

However, one should not think that what is required here is what the famous Wolff* already provided in the introductory work to his moral philosophy (which he labelled '*universal practical philosophy*'*), and that therefore we do not have to open up an entirely new field. Precisely because it was supposed to be a universal practical philosophy, it did not take into consideration a will of any particular kind, such as one that is determined completely by a priori principles without any empirical motivating grounds, and which can be called a pure will. Rather it considered willing in general,* with all the actions and conditions that belong to it in this general sense. In this way, it differs from a metaphysics of morals, just as general logic differs from transcendental philosophy: the former deals with activities and rules of thinking *in general*, while the latter deals with the particular activities and rules of *pure* thinking, i.e. of those by which objects are known completely a priori. For the metaphysics of morals should investigate the ideas and the principles of a possible *pure* will, and not the activities and conditions of human willing in general, which are for the most part drawn from psychology. It is no objection to my assertion that (without any real warrant) the 'universal practical philosophy' also talks of moral laws and duties. For on this point as well, the creators of this discipline remain true to their idea of it: they fail to distinguish between motives that are conceived of completely a priori (by reason on its own) and empirical motives (which the understanding elevates to universal concepts merely by generalizing from individual experiences). They therefore pay no attention to the difference in the sources of motives, but only to their greater or lesser strength (because they treat them as all the same). And this is how they construct their concept of *obligation*, which is anything but *moral* obligation; but this is all that can be expected from a philosophy that does not consider the *origin* of all possible practical concepts, that is, whether they arise a priori or merely a posteriori.*

Intending some day to publish a Metaphysics of Morals,* I issue this Groundwork* in advance. To be sure, there is no genuine foundation for the former other than the Critique of a *pure practical reason*,* just as for metaphysics there is the Critique of pure theoretical reason that I have already published.* But firstly, the practical Critique is not as vital as the theoretical, since when it comes to moral matters, human reason even with the least sophisticated understanding can easily be brought to a high degree of correctness and accuracy, whereas in its theoretical but pure use, it leads to irresolvable (dialectical) contradictions. And secondly, if a critique of pure practical reason is to be complete, it must be able to show its unity with theoretical reason in a common principle; because in the end there can be only one and the same reason, differing only in its application. But I could not do this here without introducing considerations of a quite different kind and confusing the reader. This is why I call this a *Groundwork for the Metaphysics of Morals*, instead of a *Critique of Pure Practical Reason*.

Thirdly, since a Metaphysics of Morals, despite its daunting title, could prove highly popular and suitable for the common understanding, I find it useful to separate from it this preparatory groundwork, so that the subtleties that cannot be avoided here can be omitted from 392 more easily comprehensible works in the future.

By contrast the present groundwork is nothing more than the identification and vindication of *the supreme principle of morality*, a project complete in itself, and separate from every other moral investigation. What I have to say about this central question—which is important, but has been neglected hitherto—would be greatly illuminated by the application of that same principle to the whole system, and greatly confirmed by the satisfactory way in which the principle performs throughout. But I had to forgo this. It would in any case have been more for my own gratification than in the general interest, since it is not a wholly reliable proof of a principle that it can be used easily and in an apparently satisfactory way; rather it arouses a bias against examining and weighing the principle strictly by itself and regardless of the consequences of using it.

I believe that the method I have adopted in this work is the most appropriate if one wants to work analytically from common knowledge of morality to the determination of its supreme principle, and back again synthetically* from the examination of this principle and its sources to common knowledge, in which we find it used. Thus the division of this work is as follows:

1. *First section*: Transition from common to philosophical rational knowledge of morality.
2. *Second section*: Transition from popular moral philosophy to the metaphysics of morals.
3. *Third section*: Final step from the metaphysics of morals to the critique of pure practical reason.

TRANSITION FROM COMMON TO
PHILOSOPHICAL RATIONAL KNOWLEDGE
OF MORALITY

IT is impossible to think of anything in the world, or indeed even outside it, that can be taken to be good without qualification, except a *good will*. *Talents* of the mind such as understanding, wit, and judgement, and qualities of *temperament* such as courage, determination, and tenacity, are doubtless in many respects good and desirable—but they can also be evil and harmful in the extreme, if the will that uses these gifts of nature, which comprise a person's *character*, is not good. The same is the case with *gifts of fortune*. Power, riches, honour, even health, and the all-round well-being and contentment with one's state that we call *happiness** make a person bold, but quite often arrogant as well, if no good will is present; the good will is needed to correct their influence on the mind, thereby correcting its whole principle of action, and fitting them for universal ends. Not to mention that a rational impartial spectator could never take satisfaction in seeing the undisturbed good fortune of a being graced with no trace of a pure and good will; hence a good will appears to be an indispensable condition even of being worthy to be happy.

Indeed, some character traits are conducive to this good will itself and can make its work much easier. But still, they have no unconditional inner worth, and always presuppose a good will, which means that the high esteem in which they are otherwise rightly held is qualified, and so it is impermissible to treat them as absolutely good. Moderation in emotions and passions, self-control and sober reflection, are not only good in many respects, but they even appear to constitute a person's *inner* worth. Nonetheless, it would be remiss to call them good without qualification (however unconditionally they have been praised by the ancients). For without the principles of a good will they can become thoroughly evil, and the composure of

394

a villain makes them not only more dangerous, but also immediately more despicable in our eyes.

The good will is not good because of what it brings about or accomplishes, through its effectiveness in attaining some intended end. Rather, it is good just through its willing, and therefore good in itself. And, just by itself, it is to be esteemed as incomparably higher than anything that could be accomplished by it merely on behalf of some inclination and indeed, if it comes to that, the sum of all inclinations. Even if, by some simple twist of fate, or poorly equipped by a stepmotherly nature, this will should completely lack the capacity to carry out its purpose; if despite its best efforts it should still accomplish nothing, and only the good will remains (though of course not as a mere wish, but as the mustering of all means that are within our power); then it would still shine like a jewel, simply for its own sake, as something that has its full worth in itself. Usefulness or fruitlessness can neither add nor detract from its worth. They would just be the setting, so to speak, not what determines its worth for those who can genuinely appreciate it, but what makes it more easily handled in our everyday transactions, or attracts the attention of those who are still lacking in genuine appreciation.

Yet there is something so strange in this idea of the absolute worth of a mere will, which is not evaluated on the basis of any usefulness, that although even common reason agrees with it, a suspicion must nevertheless arise that perhaps it is covertly grounded on a high-flown fantasy, and that we have misunderstood nature's purpose in 395 assigning reason to our will as its ruler. We will therefore examine how such an idea stands up from this perspective.

When considering how a natural being is organized to suit it to the purpose of living, we assume as a principle that each of its organs* is the most fitting and appropriate for its ends. Now if, in a being that has reason and a will, the real end of nature were its *preservation*, its *welfare*, in a word its *happiness*, then nature would have hit upon a very bad arrangement by appointing the creature's reason to accomplish this purpose. For instinct would have been better at mapping out the actions and the general rule needed for this purpose, and would thereby have attained happiness much more reliably than could ever happen through reason. If in addition reason had been bestowed upon this fortunate creature, its only role would have been to contemplate the lucky organization of its nature, to enable it to admire it, to rejoice in it, and to make it grateful to its beneficent cause; reason's role would not be to subject its faculty of desire to any feeble and deceptive guidance, and to meddle with nature's purpose. In a word, nature would have prevented reason from striking out into *practical use*, and from presuming, with its feeble insights, to devise its own plan for happiness and the means for achieving it. Nature would have taken over not only the choice of ends, but also the means, and as a wise precaution would have entrusted both of them to instinct.

In actual fact, we find that the more a cultivated reason gives itself over to the aim of enjoying life and of happiness, the more the human being departs from true contentment. As a result there arises in many people, and indeed in those most experienced in the use of reason, if only they are honest enough to admit it, a certain degree of *misology*, i.e. a hatred of reason. For after they weigh up all the advantages they derive—not just from the invention of all the arts of common luxury,* but even from the sciences (which in the end also comes to appear to them to be a luxury of the understanding)—they discover that in fact they have just burdened themselves more than they have 396 gained in happiness. As a result, they finally come to envy, rather than disdain, the common run of people, who are more closely guided by mere natural instinct, and who do not permit reason much influence over their deeds and omissions. To this extent, those who judge that we ought to greatly moderate and even abandon entirely the vainglorious eulogies about the happiness and contentment of life that reason was supposed to obtain for us do not just display moroseness or ingratitude to the goodness with which the world is governed. On the contrary, implicitly underlying these judgements is the idea of another and far worthier purpose of their existence, and towards which, rather than happiness, reason is quite properly directed; and this, as supreme, is that which for the most part must take precedence over the private aims of the human being.

As we have seen, reason is not well suited to guide the will reliably with regard to its objects and the satisfaction of all our needs (which to some extent it even multiplies)—an end to which an implanted natural instinct would have led us much more reliably. Since reason nonetheless has been imparted to us as a practical faculty—that is, as one that is meant to influence *the will*—its true function must be to produce a *will* that is *good*, not for other purposes *as a means*, but as good *in itself*. For this function, reason is absolutely necessary; here as elsewhere, nature has gone to work purposively in distributing its capacities. So although this cannot be the only and complete good, it must yet be the highest good, and the condition of everything else, even of our craving for happiness. It is therefore perfectly consistent with the wisdom of nature to recognize that the cultivation of reason, which is required for the primary and unconditional purpose of producing a good will, in many ways limits (at least in this life) the attainment of happiness, and makes of it a subordinate purpose that is always conditioned; indeed reason can reduce happiness to less than nothing without nature thereby undermining its own purposes. This is because, even if it should infringe greatly on the inclinations, reason recognizes its highest practical vocation to lie in the grounding of the good will, and hence is capable of its own distinctive form of satisfaction from fulfilling an end that only it itself has determined.

397   But we now have to further elucidate the concept of a will that is estimable in itself and good apart from any further purpose. This concept already dwells in natural sound understanding and needs not so much to be taught as just brought to light. It always holds the highest place in estimating the whole worth of our actions, and it constitutes the condition of everything else. To elucidate it, we shall put before us the concept of *duty*, which contains that of the good will, but under certain subjective limitations and hindrances; however, far from concealing it and making it unrecognizable, this rather brings it out by contrast and makes it shine more brightly.

In considering the concept of duty, I leave aside all actions that, even though they might be useful for this or that purpose, are clearly contrary to duty; for in their case the question of whether they might have been done *from duty* does not even arise, since they actually conflict with it. I also set aside actions that in fact conform with duty, but for which human beings have *no inclination* immediately, and which nonetheless they still perform because driven to do so by another inclination. In this case it is easy to distinguish whether the action that conforms with duty was done *from duty* or from a selfish purpose. It is much more difficult to see this difference when an action conforms with duty, and the subject also has an *immediate* inclination towards it. As an example of the easier case, it certainly *conforms* with duty that a shopkeeper not overcharge their inexperienced customers; and, where there is a lot of trade, a shrewd merchant will not do this, but will charge everyone the same prices, so that even a child may buy from them just like anyone else. As a result everyone is served *honestly*. But we should not think that the merchant has acted *from* duty and from *principles* of honesty: rather, it was to their advantage. Likewise, we should not suppose that in addition, the merchant had an immediate inclination towards their customers—like love, so to speak—to give no one preferential treatment. Thus the action was done neither from duty, nor from immediate inclination, but merely for a self-interested purpose.

As an example of the more difficult case, by contrast: to preserve one's life is a duty, and besides everyone has an immediate inclination to do so. But as a result, the often anxious care which the greatest part of humanity takes over this nonetheless has no inner worth, and their maxim no moral content. They certainly protect their lives *in conformity with duty*, but not *from duty*. If, on the other hand, adversity and inconsolable grief have entirely taken away the taste for life; if this unfortunate person, strong in soul, and more incensed at their fate than despondent or dejected, wishes for death; and yet preserves their life without loving it—not from inclination or fear but from duty—then indeed their maxim has moral content.

Another example: to be beneficent where one can is a duty; and besides many souls are of such a sympathetic character that even without a motivating ground of vanity, or of self-interest, they find an inner gratification in spreading pleasure around them, and take delight in the pleasure of others—insofar as they have brought it about. But I claim that such actions, however far they conform with duty, however amiable they may be, still have no true moral worth. Rather, this is on a par with other inclinations, such as the inclination for honour, which if fortunate enough to hit upon what is in fact in the public interest and in conformity with duty, and as a result is actually honourable, deserves praise and encouragement but not high esteem. For the maxim lacks moral content, since such actions are to be done not from inclination, but *from duty*.

Suppose, then, that the mind of this friend of humanity were so clouded over by their own grief that all their sympathetic concern for the fate of others were extinguished, and that they still have the means to help others in need, but these needs do not move them because they are sufficiently occupied with their own. Suppose now that, though inclination no longer stimulates them to help others, they were nonetheless to tear themselves out of this deadly insensibility, and to do the action without any inclination but from duty—not until then does the action have genuine moral worth. Still further: if nature had placed little sympathy in the heart of this or that person; even if (though otherwise honest) they were by temperament cold and indifferent to the sufferings of others, perhaps because they are endowed with the special gift of patience and endurance towards their own suffering, and presuppose or even require the same in everyone else; if nature had not fashioned such a person to be a friend of humanity, though they would not be its worst product—might they not nonetheless find in themselves a source from which to give themselves a far higher worth than that which may belong to a good-natured temperament? Certainly! This is precisely where the worth of character arises, which is moral and beyond all comparison the highest, namely being beneficent not from inclination, but from duty.

399

A final example: to secure one's own happiness is a duty (at least indirectly); for in a crowd of many troubles and amidst unsatisfied needs, lack of contentment with one's condition could easily become a great *temptation to transgress one's duties*. But, even independently of this duty, all human beings already have the most powerful and deeply felt inclination to happiness, as this is precisely the idea that all inclinations are satisfied together. However, while the prescription of happiness usually infringes greatly on some inclinations, at the same time human beings cannot arrive at any determinate and reliable concept of the sum of satisfaction under the name of happiness. It is therefore not surprising that a single inclination, if it is determinate in regard to what it promises and the time in which its satisfaction can be obtained, is able to outweigh a wavering idea. It can thus happen that a human being, for example someone with gout, may choose to enjoy what they fancy and to suffer as much as they can bear, since as they see it, they have at least not denied themselves the enjoyment of the present moment, for what might be a groundless expectation of some good fortune that is meant to lie in health. But once again in this case, if the universal inclination towards happiness is not what determines the person's will, if health has not entered into their calculations as being necessary, nevertheless here, as in all other cases, a law still remains, namely to promote one's happiness not from inclination but from duty; and only then does the person's conduct finally have genuine moral worth.

It is in this way, no doubt, that we are to understand the passages from Scripture which command us to love our neighbour and even our enemy. For love as an inclination cannot be commanded; but beneficence based on duty, even if not driven by any inclination whatsoever (indeed even if natural and unconquerable aversion resists), is *practical* and not *pathological* love. This love resides in the will and not feeling, in the principles of action, and not in melting compassion; but only as the former can it be commanded.

The second proposition* is this: an action from duty has its moral worth *not in the purpose* that is to be attained by it, but rather in the maxim according to which it is decided upon. That worth therefore does not depend on the realization of the object of the action, but merely on the *principle of willing* according to which the action is done, without regard for any object of the faculty of desire. It is clear from what was said previously that the purposes we may have when we act, and their effects, considered as ends and drivers* of the will, cannot bestow unconditional and moral worth on actions. In what, then, can this worth lie, if it is not in the will and its relation to the hoped-for effect? It can lie nowhere else *than in the principle of the will*, regardless of the ends that can be brought about by such action. For the will stands as it were at a cross-roads, between its *a priori* principle, which is formal, and its *a posteriori* drive, which is material; and because it must be determined by something, when an action is done from duty, it will have to be determined by the formal principle of willing as such, since every material principle has been taken away from it.

The third proposition, as the conclusion from both previous ones, I would express as follows: *duty is the necessity of an action out of respect*

for the law.* When I have some action in mind, I can have an *inclination* for the object that I would bring about, but never *respect*, precisely because it is merely the *effect*, and not the *activity* of a will. Likewise, I cannot have respect for inclination as such, whether it is mine or someone else's; at most, when it is mine, I can approve of it, and when it is someone else's, I can sometimes love it myself, as favourable to my own advantage. Only that which is connected to my will merely as a ground, never as an effect; which does not serve my inclination, but outweighs it, or at least excludes it entirely from calculations when we make a choice, and hence the mere law by itself—only this can be an object of respect and hence a command. An action done from duty must entirely set aside the influence of inclination, and with it every object of the will. Thus nothing remains that could determine the will except, objectively, the *law* and subjectively, *pure respect* for this prac-
401 tical law, and hence the maxim[1] of complying with such a law, even to the detriment of all my inclinations.

Thus the moral worth of an action lies neither in the effect that is expected from it, nor therefore in a principle of action that needs to borrow its motive from this expected effect. For all these effects (such as one's own comforts, or even the advancement of the happiness of others) could have been brought about in other ways. So to achieve them, the will of a rational being is not required; but nevertheless in this will, and in it alone, can the highest and unconditional good be found. Therefore the pre-eminent good that we call moral can consist in nothing other than the *representation of the law* in itself—which obviously only occurs in the rational being—insofar as this representation, and not the hoped-for effect, is the motive of the will. This good is already present in the person who acts according to this representation; it need not wait upon the effect of their action.[2]

[1] A *maxim* is the subjective principle of willing. The objective principle (i.e. the one that would also serve all rational beings as their subjective practical principle if reason had complete control over the faculty of desire) is the practical *law*.
[2] It might be objected that rather than dealing with this question clearly by using a concept of reason, in using the word '*respect*' I have instead just sought refuge behind an obscure feeling. However, although respect is a feeling, it is not one *induced* by external influence, but one that is *self-generated* through a rational concept; it is therefore specifically distinguished from all feelings of the former kind, which amount to either inclination or fear. What I recognize immediately as a law for myself I recognize with respect, which

But what kind of law can this possibly be, where for the will to be   402
called good absolutely and without qualification, the representation
of the law must determine the will regardless of any expected result?
Since I have robbed the will of every impetus that could arise for it
from following some particular law, the only thing remaining that
could serve the will as its principle is the universal conformity of
actions to law as such. That is, I ought never to proceed except in
such a way *that I could also will that my maxim become a universal law*.
Here, then, what serves the will as its principle is mere conformity
with law as such (without any law concerning particular actions serv-
ing as its ground); and this must be the case if duty is not to be an
empty delusion and a chimerical concept. In making its practical
judgments, common human reason actually agrees with this principle,
and has it constantly in view.

For example, the question might be this: May I, when hard pressed,
make a promise with the intention of not keeping it? Here it is easy
for me to distinguish the different meanings the question can have:
whether to make a false promise is prudent; or whether it accords
with duty. Making a false promise can, no doubt, often be prudent.
Of course, I can see perfectly well that this subterfuge might not get
me out of my tricky situation, as in addition I should think carefully
about whether this lie may not give me even greater trouble later on.
Thus, one might act *more prudently* in this matter by proceeding according to a universal maxim, and by making it one's habit to promise
nothing except when one intends to keep it; for, the consequences of

---

just means the consciousness of the *subordination* of my will under a law, without the
mediation of any other influences. The immediate determination of the will by the law,
and the awareness of that determination, is called *respect*, so that it is viewed as the *effect*
of the law on the subject and not as its *cause*. Actually, respect is the representation of
a worth that demolishes my self-love. Thus it is something that is considered an object
neither of inclination, nor of fear, even though it is at the same time somewhat analogous
to both. The sole *object* of respect is the *law*—which we impose on *ourselves* and yet which
is necessary in itself. We are subject to it as a law, without self-love being consulted; as
imposed upon ourselves, it is nevertheless a consequence of our will. In the first regard,
it is analogous to fear, in the second to inclination. All respect for a person is actually only
respect for the law (for righteousness etc.), which they exemplify. Because we also regard
the expansion of our talents as a duty, we represent a person of talents as also *exemplifying
a law*, as it were (to emulate them in this way through practice), and this is what constitutes our respect for them. All so-called moral *interest* consists solely in *respect* for law.

all my supposed *cunning* are not so easy to foresee, and once trust in me is lost, this may be worse than the evil that I now mean to avoid. Only it soon becomes clear to me that a maxim of this sort will still just be based on fear of the consequences. However, to be truthful from duty is quite different from being truthful from fear of adverse consequences. In the former case, the concept of the action in itself already contains a law for me, whereas in the latter I must first look around elsewhere to see how things are likely to turn out for me. Even

403 though deserting my maxim of prudence can sometimes be very advantageous to me (though adhering to it is of course safer), it is quite certainly wicked to deviate from the principle of duty. If I seek the quickest accurate way of answering the question whether a lying promise conforms with duty then I ask myself: would I really be content that my maxim (namely, of getting myself out of my tricky situation by means of a lying promise) should hold as a universal law (for myself as well as others)? And would I be able to say to myself: everyone may make a lying promise if they find themselves in a situation they can get out of in no other way? I then immediately see that while I can will the lie, I cannot will a *universal law* to lie. For if there were such a law, there would actually be no promise at all: it would be futile for me to declare my future intentions to those who would not believe me—or if they were rash enough to do so, would pay me back in the same way. Hence my maxim, as soon as it were made a universal law, would necessarily destroy itself.

Thus I do not need any penetrating or astute intelligence to see how to make my willing morally good. Inexperienced in the way of the world, and unprepared for whatever lies in store, I only ask myself: can you also will that your maxim become universal law? If not, then it is to be discarded; not because of the prospect of some cost to you or others, but because it cannot serve as a principle in any possible universal lawgiving, for which reason compels immediate respect. And even if I have not yet *fathomed* its grounds (something the philosopher may investigate), I at least understand this much: it involves the apprehension of a worth that far outweighs anything extolled by inclination; and that what constitutes duty is the necessity of my actions from *pure* respect for the practical law to which, as the condition of a will good in itself, the worth of which surpasses everything else, any other motivating ground must give way.

Thus, we have now reached the principle of the moral knowledge of common human reason, which it admittedly does not think of in the universal form into which we have distilled it, but does always have before its eyes and uses as a standard for judging. It would be 404 easy to show how common human reason, with this compass in its hand, knows very well how to distinguish in any case that arises what is good from what is evil, what conforms to duty or is contrary to it. Without attempting to teach it anything new, reason just has to be made to attend to its own principle, as it was by Socrates. Thus neither science nor philosophy is needed to know what one has to do in order to be honest and good, indeed even to be wise and virtuous. It should have been obvious all along that the knowledge of what all human beings are under an obligation to do and to know is the business of everyone, even the commonest. In this respect one cannot help but admire the great advantage that in the human understanding, the capacity for practical judgement has over its theoretical counterpart. In the latter, when common reason dares to depart from the laws of experience and the perceptions of the senses, it falls into sheer incomprehensibility or internal contradiction, or at least into a chaos of uncertainty, obscurity, and vacillation. But in practical matters, it is precisely when common understanding excludes all sensuous drives from practical laws that the power of judging first begins to show itself to advantage. The common understanding then even acquires a certain sophistication — perhaps in quibbling with its conscience or with other claims about what is 'right', or instead trying honestly to determine the worth of actions for its own instruction. The crucial thing is that when it does try honestly, common understanding is just as likely as any philosopher to hit the mark. Indeed, the common understanding is almost *more* likely to do so than the philosopher, because the latter must operate with the same principle as the former; but the philosopher can easily confuse their judgement with a host of alien and irrelevant considerations and so be deflected from the right path. As a result, would it not be wiser to leave moral matters to the judgement of common reason, and just call in philosophy to present morals in a more systematic and graspable form, and make its rules easier to apply (and also to debate)—but when it comes to practical matters, prevent philosophy putting common human reason on a new path of investigation and instruction, and leading it away from its fortunate simplicity?

405   Innocence is a wonderful thing, but sadly it is so hard to preserve and so easy to seduce. Because of this, even wisdom—which otherwise is more a matter of conduct than of reflective knowing—still needs rational inquiry too, not in order to learn from it, but in order to make sure that what wisdom prescribes is effective and enduring. From their needs and inclinations, the entire satisfaction of which they sum up under the name of happiness, human beings feel within themselves a powerful counterweight to all those commands of duty that reason represents as so deserving of the highest respect. Now reason issues its commands unrelentingly, yet without promising anything to the inclinations, and hence, as it were, disrespecting and disregarding those claims, which are so impetuous and yet which seem so reasonable (and are not willing to be suppressed by any command). But from this there arises a *natural dialectic:** namely, a propensity to rationalize against those strict laws of duty, to cast doubt on their validity, or at least their purity and strictness, and where possible, to make them more amenable to our wishes and inclinations. This is to fundamentally corrupt these laws and to deprive them of all their dignity, something that even common practical reason cannot ultimately endorse.

    As a result, *common human reason* is compelled to leave its sphere, not by some idle speculative need (the like of which never troubles it as long as it is content to be mere sound reason), but rather on practical grounds. It then steps into the field of a *practical philosophy*, in order to gain information and instruction about the source and correct determination of its principle—in opposition to maxims based on need and inclination. In this way it may escape from the predicament of competing claims, and not run the risk of being deprived of all genuine moral principles because of the equivocation into which it easily falls. Thus even practical common reason, when cultivated, inadvertently gives rise to a *dialectic* requiring it to seek for help from philosophy, just as it does in its theoretical use. The one will find as little peace as the other except through a complete critique of pure reason.

SECTION II

TRANSITION FROM POPULAR MORAL PHILOSOPHY TO THE METAPHYSICS OF MORALS

IF so far we have drawn our concept of duty from the common use of our practical reason, it should by no means be concluded that we have thereby treated it as a concept of experience. On the contrary, if we consider our experience of human conduct, we come upon the frequent and (as we ourselves admit) justifiable complaint that no certain example can be cited of the disposition to act from pure duty. For, though many actions *conform* with what *duty* commands, it is still always doubtful whether an action is actually done *from duty* and thus has a moral worth. That is why there have always been philosophers who have absolutely denied the reality of this disposition in human actions, and attributed everything to a more or less refined self-love. However, those philosophers have not called into doubt the correctness of the concept of morality as a result. Rather, they have spoken with deep regret of the frailty and impurity of a human nature that has enough nobility to take an idea so worthy of respect as its rule, but is at the same time too weak to follow it. It thus uses reason, which should serve as its law giver, only to further the interests of our inclinations, whether individually or as a whole.

In actual fact, it is absolutely impossible for experience to identify with complete certainty a single case in which the maxim of an action that otherwise conforms with duty was based exclusively on moral grounds and on the recognition of one's duty. There are indeed cases where even the most searching self-examination finds nothing other than duty which could have been powerful enough to move us to this or that good action or this and that great sacrifice. Nonetheless, it cannot be concluded with certainty that the real determining cause of the will was not actually some secret impulse of self-love, under the guise of the idea of duty. So while we like to flatter ourselves with false pretensions to a nobler motive, in fact we can never, even with the most searching self-examination, bring entirely to light what secretly drives us. For, when moral worth is at issue, what counts is not the actions which one sees, but their inner principles, which one does not.*

Furthermore, there is no better way to play into the hands of those who ridicule morality as a mere figment of our imagination puffing itself up through self-conceit, than by conceding to them that the concepts of duty must be drawn solely from experience (just as we find it all too easy to believe of all other concepts). By doing so, one paves the way for their inevitable victory. Out of love of humanity, I am willing to concede that most of our actions conform to duty. But were we to look more closely at our scheming and striving, we would everywhere run into the dear self, which always comes to the fore; and it is this self, rather than the strict command of duty—which in many cases would require self-denial—that underpins our intentions. One need not be an enemy of virtue, but just a dispassionate observer who does not immediately equate wanting to be good, however strongly, with being good, to then doubt on occasion whether any true virtue is to be found in the world at all. (Such moments come particularly with advancing years and a power of judgement that experience has made both wiser and more acute.) At this point, the only thing that can prevent us completely abandoning our ideas of duty, or preserve in our souls a well-founded respect for its law, is the following clear conviction: that, even if no actions have ever flowed from such pure 408 sources, what matters is not what does or does not *in fact* happen, but rather whether reason by itself and independently of all appearances commands what *ought to* happen. Hence reason unrelentingly commands actions of which the world so far has perhaps not yet provided any example, and the feasibility of which would be highly dubious if experience were taken to be the foundation of everything. For example, genuine honesty in friendship is no less required of each person even if up to now there has never been an honest friend, because this duty is a duty as such, prior to all experience, which rests on the idea of reason determining the will on a priori grounds.

In addition, unless one wants to deny to the concept of morality truth and applicability to any possible object, one cannot dispute that its law is so extensive in its significance that it must hold, not merely for human beings, but for *all rational beings as such,* and thus not merely under contingent conditions and with exceptions, but with *absolute necessity.* Clearly, then, it is not on the basis of experience that one can conclude that such absolutely certain and necessary laws are even possible. For by what right can we make what is perhaps valid only under the contingent conditions of humanity into an object of unqualified respect, as a universal prescription for every rational nature? And how could laws for the determination of *our* will be taken as laws for the determination of the will of a rational being as such (and only thereby laws for our will as well), if they were merely empirical, and did not originate completely a priori in pure, but nonetheless practical, reason?

Moreover, one could not do morality a worse service than by trying to derive it from examples. For every purported example of morality would first have to be judged according to principles of morality, to see whether it is actually worthy to serve as a foundation, i.e. as a model—examples can in no way supply us with the concept of morality in the first place. Even the Holy One of the Gospel must first be compared with our ideal of moral perfection before he is recognized as such. He even says of himself: 'Why do you call me (whom you see) good? No one is good (the archetype of the good), but God alone (whom you do not see)'.* But from where do we get the concept of God as the highest good? Solely from the *idea* of moral perfection 409 that reason devises a priori, and connects inseparably with the concept of a free will. Imitating others has no place at all in moral matters, and examples only play the role of encouragement. That is, they put the feasibility of what the law commands beyond doubt, and they make intuitive what the practical rule expresses in more general terms. But they can never entitle us to set aside their true original, which lies in reason, and instead to follow examples.

If then, the only genuine supreme principle of morality rests on pure reason independently of all experience, it should be unnecessary even to ask whether it is a good thing to set forth these concepts in the abstract. For these concepts, along with their associated principles, are established a priori, insofar as this knowledge is to differ from common knowledge and to be properly called philosophical. But in our day and age, it might be necessary to ask this question after all. For if one were to take a vote between on the one hand pure rational knowledge separated off from anything empirical (hence metaphysics of morals), and on the other hand popular practical philosophy,* it is easy to guess on which side the majority would fall.

Descending to the level of popular concepts is certainly highly commendable, but only if our ascent to the principles of pure reason has already taken place and been accomplished to complete satisfaction; that is, first *grounding* the doctrine of morals on metaphysics, and then afterwards making it *accessible* by giving it a popular character. But it hardly makes sense to aim at popularity in this first inquiry, upon which the very correctness of the principles depends. It is not just that such a procedure can never lay claim to the extremely rare merit of truly *philosophical* popularity (after all, it takes no skill to be understood by all and sundry when one renounces insight into the heart of things). It also produces a revolting mish-mash of cobbled-together observations and half-baked principles, which shallow minds lap up because it is useful in everyday chatter. The more insightful, however, feel confused and avert their eyes, with a dissatisfaction that nonetheless they are unable to cure. Yet philosophers, who can perfectly well see through this deception, do not get a hearing when they 410 call off would-be popularizing for a while, until it can earn the *right* to be popular by first acquiring genuine insight.

We need only look at essays on morality in this popularizing style to find a wondrous jumble: now the special function of human nature (though occasionally with reference to the idea of a rational nature as such), now perfection, now happiness, here moral feeling, there fear of God, a bit of this and a bit of that. However, it does not occur to anyone to ask if we should be looking for the principles of morality in our knowledge of human nature at all (which after all, we can only get from experience). And if we should not—if these principles are to be found completely a priori, free from anything empirical, simply in pure rational concepts and not even to the slightest extent elsewhere—then we should decide instead to conduct this investigation entirely separately as a pure practical philosophy; or (if one may use a name that is so vilified) a metaphysics[1] of morals. This

---

[1] If one wants, one can distinguish *pure* moral philosophy (metaphysics of morals) from *applied* morals (namely, as applied to human nature)—just as one can distinguish between pure and applied mathematics, and pure and applied logic in a similar way.

would be enough to complete the investigation by itself, and put off a public that demands popularity until this undertaking has been concluded.

But a completely isolated metaphysics of morals, which is not mixed up with anthropology, theology, physics, or hyperphysics, and still less with occult qualities (which one might call hypophysical), is not just an indispensable basis for all clearly defined theoretical knowledge of ethics; at the same time, it is fundamental for the actual implementation of its dictates. For if it is not mixed with the alien addition of empirical inducements, the pure representation of duty— and in general of the moral law, through reason alone (which in this way for the first time becomes aware that, by itself, it can also be practical)—has an influence on the human heart that is so much more powerful than all the other drives[1] which can be summoned 411 from the empirical field. As a result, reason, aware of its own dignity, regards these drives with contempt, and little by little it can master them. The alternative is a mixed doctrine of morals, with drives from feeling and inclination put alongside rational concepts, which will inevitably cause the mind to waver between motives that can be brought under no principle, and that by sheer chance can guide us to the good, but also quite often to what is evil.

From what has been said so far, it is clear that, *firstly*, all moral concepts have their seat and origin in reason completely a priori, and indeed just as much in the commonest human reason as in that which

Moreover, by using this label one is immediately reminded that moral principles are not grounded in the peculiarities of human nature, but must exist a priori by themselves, and that from such principles it must be possible to derive practical rules for every rational nature, and as a result for human nature as well.

[1] The admirable late Professor Sulzer* has sent me a letter, in which he asks me why the teachings of virtue, however convincing they are to reason, accomplish so little. My reply has been delayed, because I wanted to make it complete. It is just this: the teachers themselves have not purified their concepts, and they overdo things by grabbing motives for moral goodness from all over the place; in their attempt to make their medicine so strong, they spoil it. For even the most common observation shows that a righteous action—one performed with a steadfast soul, without aiming at any advantage, in this world or another, even under the greatest temptations of need, or enticement—when presented to us then far surpasses and eclipses any otherwise similar action at all affected by an alien drive, also elevates the soul, and stirs up the wish to be able to act like that too. Even reasonably young children feel this impression, and one should never present duties to them in any other way.

is speculative to the highest degree. *Secondly*, these concepts cannot be derived by abstraction from any knowledge that is empirical and hence merely contingent. *Thirdly*, their worthiness to serve us as pure practical principles lies precisely in this purity of their origin. *Fourthly*, whenever anything empirical is added to them, just as much is taken away from their genuine influence and from the unqualified worth of the corresponding actions. *Fifthly*, it is not only of the utmost necessity for theoretical purposes, when our concern is only speculative, but it is also a matter of the greatest practical importance that we derive morality's concepts and laws from pure reason, and so set them out pure and unmixed; and likewise to determine the scope of this entire practical but pure sphere of rational knowledge, i.e. of the whole faculty of pure practical reason. But in doing this, we must not make morality's principles dependent on the particular nature of human reason (as speculative philosophy may well permit, and indeed

412   even at times find necessary). Rather, since moral laws are to hold for every rational being as such, they already derive from the universal concept of a rational being as such. Thus we should be able to set out the whole of moral theory—which, although it needs anthropology for its application to human beings, is nonetheless an entirely separate type of knowledge—first of all independently, as pure philosophy, i.e. as metaphysics. Without metaphysics it might be possible to determine precisely (for purposes of speculative judgement) the moral element of duty in all actions which accord with duty; nonetheless, it would be impossible to found morality on genuine principles without metaphysics, even for merely common and practical use, particularly for moral training to bring about pure moral dispositions and to graft them onto people's minds, for the sake of the world's highest good.

Advancing by natural stages, this work will proceed not merely from *common moral judgement* (which is treated here with great respect) to what is *philosophical*, as has already been done, but also from a *popular philosophy* (which gets as far as groping around with examples can take it) to *metaphysics* (which does not let itself be held back any further by anything empirical; and because it must survey the whole of this kind of rational knowledge, may have to extend itself to *ideas*,* where examples desert us). For this to be achieved, we must trace and clearly present the faculty of practical reason, from the general rules by which it is determined right up to the point where the concept of duty arises from it.

Everything in nature works according to laws. But only a rational being has the capacity to act according to the *representation* of laws, i.e. according to principles, and so only such a being has a *will*. Since *reason* is required for deriving actions from laws, the will is nothing other than practical reason. If a being has a will that is unfailingly determined by reason then, when it recognizes actions as objectively necessary, they are also subjectively necessary; that is, the will is the capacity to choose *only that* which reason, independently of inclination, recognizes to be practically necessary, i.e. as good. However, if reason just by itself does not sufficiently determine the will, it may also be subject to subjective conditions (i.e. to certain drives) that are not always in agreement with objective conditions. In a word, 413 if the will does not *in itself* completely conform with reason—as is actually the case with human beings—then actions that are recognized as objectively necessary are subjectively contingent. Then the determination of such a will, in conformity with objective laws, is *necessitation*: that is, the relation of objective laws to a will not altogether good is represented as the determination of the will of a rational being on the basis of reason, but in such a way that, given its nature, it is not always obedient to it.

The representation of an objective principle insofar as it is necessitating for a will is called a command (of reason), and the way this command is formulated is called an *imperative*.

All imperatives are expressed by an *ought*, thereby showing that here the objective law of reason relates to a will that, given its subjective constitution, is not necessarily determined by it (that is, the law necessitates). Such imperatives say that to do or to omit something would be good; but they say it to a will that does not always do what is represented to it as good. Nonetheless, the practically *good* determines the will by means of representations of reason, hence not from subjective causes, but objectively, i.e. from grounds that are valid for every rational being as such. This good is distinguishable from the *agreeable*, which influences the will only by means of sensation from merely subjective causes, and holds for the senses of this person or that, but not as a principle of reason, which holds for everyone.[1]

414   Thus a perfectly good will would stand just as much under objective laws (of the good); but that does not mean that it can thereby be conceived as *necessitated* to actions that conform with laws. For, because of the way it is subjectively constituted, it can only be determined to act by the representation of the good. As a result, no imperatives hold for the *divine* will or the *holy* will in general: here the '*ought*' is out of place, because the *willing* is already by itself necessarily in agreement with the law. Therefore imperatives are only formulations that express the relation of objective laws of willing as such to the subjective imperfection of the will of some rational being or other, e.g. of the human will.

Now, all *imperatives* command either *hypothetically*, or *categorically*. The former represent a possible action as practically necessary as a means to achieving something else that one wants (or may want). By contrast, the *categorical* imperative would represent* the action as objectively necessary in itself, without reference to another end.

Every practical law represents a possible action as good and hence as necessary for a subject whose actions can be practically determined by reason. As a result, all imperatives are formulations that determine an action that is necessary according to the principle of a will that is good in some way. Now, if the action would be good merely as a means to *something else*, the imperative is *hypothetical*; if the action is represented

---

[1] Where the faculty of desire depends on sensation, it is called inclination, which therefore always shows there is a *need*. But the dependence of a contingently determinable will on principles of reason is called an *interest*. Hence an interest is only found within a dependent will which of itself does not always conform with reason; in the divine will, interest is inconceivable. But even the human will can *take* an *interest* in something without therefore *acting from interest*; the former signifies the *practical* interest in the action, the latter the *pathological* interest in the object of the action. Taking an interest indicates only dependence of the will on principles of reason by itself, whereas acting from interest indicates dependence on its principles for the sake of inclination, namely when reason only supplies the practical rule as a way to satisfy the need of inclination. In the former what interests me is the action; in the latter what interests me is the object of the action (insofar as it is agreeable to me). We already saw in the first section that in an action from duty one must pay attention not to the interest in the object, but merely to the interest in the action itself and its principle in reason (the law).

as good *in itself*, hence as necessary in a will that in itself conforms to reason as its principle, then the imperative is *categorical*.

The imperative thus says which of my possible actions would be good, and represents the practical rule as related to a will that does not immediately perform an action just because it is good (maybe because the subject does not always know that it is good, or because their maxims could still be opposed to the objective principles of a practical reason even if they did know this).

The hypothetical imperative thus says only that the action is good for some *possible* or *actual* purpose. In the first case it is a *problematically* practical principle, in the second an *assertorically* practical principle. 415 The categorical imperative declares the action to be objectively *necessary* of itself without reference to some purpose, i.e. apart from any other end. It thus holds as an *apodictically* practical principle.*

Whatever is possible only through the powers of some rational being may also be thought of as a possible purpose for some will. Therefore if principles of action are thought of as necessary for attaining some possible purpose to be realized by it, they are in fact infinitely many. All sciences have some practical part whose task consists in making some end possible for us, and whose imperatives concern how it is to be attained. These can therefore be called imperatives of *skill*. The question does not arise here whether the end is rational and good, but only what one must do in order to attain it. To the extent that each serves to bring about its purpose perfectly, the prescriptions that the physician uses to completely cure a man, and those a poisoner uses to be sure of killing him, are of equal worth. Since in early youth it is not known what ends life might throw up, parents above all seek to have their children learn *a wide range of things*, and take care that they develop *skill* in the use of means applicable to a *variety* of ends they might or might not choose, not knowing for sure whether any of these ends will in fact become the purpose of their pupil, though it is entirely *possible* that they might. Parents can be so taken up with this approach, that they commonly fail to shape and correct their children's judgements about the worth of things that they might make their ends.

Even so, there is *one* end that can be assumed to hold for all rational beings (insofar as imperatives apply to them at all, namely as dependent beings), and thus one purpose that they not merely *can* have, but which we can safely assume they one and all actually *do have* necessarily by nature—and that is *happiness*. The hypothetical imperative that presents the practical necessity of an action as a means to further happiness is *assertoric*. It must be put forward as necessary not just to some uncertain, merely possible purpose, but to a purpose that one can safely presuppose on an a priori basis for every human being because it belongs to their essence. Now, skill in the choice of the means to one's own greatest well-being can be called *prudence* in the narrowest sense.[1] Thus an imperative that concerns the choice of means to one's own happiness, i.e. the prescription of prudence, is still *hypothetical*, as the action is not commanded in its own right but just as a means to another purpose.

Lastly, there is one imperative that commands a certain line of conduct directly, without presupposing as its condition any other purpose to be attained by that conduct. This imperative is *categorical*. It is not concerned with the matter of the action or what may result from it, but the form and the principle from which the action follows; and what is essentially good in the action consists in the disposition behind it, whatever the result happens to be. This imperative may be called the imperative of *morality*.

The ways in which willing can be based on these three principles can also be sharply distinguished through the *different ways* they necessitate the will. To make this clear it would be best if we were to call them *rules* of skill, *counsels* of prudence, and *commands* (*laws*) of morality respectively. For only *law* carries with it the concept of an *unconditional* and indeed objective and hence universally valid *necessity*; and commands are laws that must be obeyed, i.e. must be complied with even contrary to inclination. Admittedly, there is also necessity involved in giving counsel; but it can only hold under a subjective contingent condition, namely if this or that person counts

---

[1] The word 'prudence' is used in two ways: in one it refers to worldly wisdom, in the other to personal wisdom. The first is the skill of influencing others so as to use them for one's purposes. The second is the insight necessary to combine all one's own purposes to one's own lasting advantage. The worth of worldly wisdom depends on personal wisdom: someone who is worldly wise, but not personally wise, is better characterized as clever and crafty, and yet on the whole unwise.

this or that as belonging to their happiness. By contrast, the categorical imperative is qualified by no condition, and so can quite properly
be called a *command* as it is absolutely and yet practically necessary.
Imperatives of the first kind could also be called *technical* (concerned
with skill); of the second *pragmatic*[1] (concerned with well-being); and   417
of the third *moral* (belonging to free conduct as such, i.e. to morals).

Now the question arises: how are all these imperatives possible?*
Answering this question is not a matter of knowing how to carry out
the action that the imperative commands, but simply how the *necessitation* of the will that the imperative expresses in relation to some task
is to be understood. How an imperative of skill is possible calls for no
great discussion. Whoever wills the end also wills the necessary
means—at least insofar as reason has a decisive influence on their
action, and the means are under their control. When it comes to the
will, this proposition is analytic.* For thinking about what it is to will
an object, as something I bring about as an effect, already contains my
role as a cause which acts, i.e. uses means. Thus the imperative merely
unpacks the concept of actions necessary to this end from the concept
of a willing of this end. (Of course synthetic propositions are required
to determine the specific means that will be needed to achieve an
intended purpose, but they are concerned with how to bring the
object about, not the ground of the act of will as such.) It is certainly
the case that mathematics teaches, using just synthetic propositions,
that to divide a line reliably into two equal parts I must make two
intersecting arcs from its extremities. But it is an analytic proposition
that, when I know the effect I have in mind can only come about
through such an action, then if I really will the effect I also will the
action it requires. For it is one and the same thing to think of something as an effect that can be brought about by me in a certain way,
and of myself acting to bring it about in this way.

If it were only equally easy to come up with a definite concept of
happiness, then imperatives of prudence would coincide completely

[1] In my view, the word *pragmatic* can be best understood in this way. For the term
'pragmatic' is applied to *sanctions* that do not arise from the right of states as necessary
laws, but from the *precautions* they take for general well-being. Likewise a *history* is written pragmatically when it makes us *prudent*, i.e. instructs the world on how it can exploit
its advantages better than, or at least as well as, former times.

with those of skill, and be just as analytic. For in both cases it could be said: whoever wills the end also (necessarily, in accordance with rea-
418   son) wills the only means to it that are in their power. But unfortunately, the concept of happiness is so indeterminate that even though every human being wishes to attain it, yet they can never say precisely and consistently what they actually wish for or want. The reason is this: on the one hand, the elements that belong to the concept of happiness are one and all empirical, and so must be derived from experience; but on the other hand, the idea of happiness requires an absolute whole, in the sense of greatest possible well-being both now and in the future. However, a finite being, even the most insightful and capable, cannot come up with a clear idea of what it is they actually want in these circumstances. They may want riches; but then, how much worry, envy, and intrigue might they not thereby bring on themselves! They may want knowledge and insight; but that might just make them all the more terrifyingly aware of the ills that they do not yet know about, but which they cannot avoid; or might just burden their desires (which already give them enough trouble) with yet more needs. They may want long life; but who will guarantee them that it would not be a long misery? They may simply want health; but has not bodily discomfort often saved people from the kind of excess they would have plunged into had they had perfect health? And so on. In short, they cannot follow any principle to determine with complete certainty what would make them truly happy, because that would require omniscience.

One therefore cannot act on determinate principles in order to be happy, but just on advice based on experience, concerning diet, thrift, politeness, restraint, and so on, which practice tells us generally advances well-being. From this it follows that strictly speaking, the imperatives of prudence cannot *command* at all, i.e. present actions objectively as practically *necessary*. That is, they are to be taken as advice rather than as commands of reason. This is because the problem of determining reliably and universally which action would advance the happiness of a rational being cannot be solved; hence there can be no such imperative that would command us in a strict sense concerning what makes us happy. For happiness is not an ideal of reason, but of the imagination, which rests on merely empirical grounds. It is therefore hopeless to

expect such imperatives to pick out an action through which the total-   419
ity of what is in fact an infinite series of consequences could be
attained. However, this imperative of prudence would be an analytic
proposition if the means to happiness could be reliably stated, as it
only differs from an imperative of skill insofar as with an imperative of
skill the end is merely possible, while with happiness it is a given. But
still in both cases the imperative that commands willing the means
when one wills the end is analytic, since both merely command the
means to what is presupposed as the end. Thus there is also no difficulty with regard to the possibility of this sort of imperative either.

By contrast, the only question that needs to be answered is without
doubt how the imperative of *morality* is possible, since it is not a hypothetical imperative at all; and thus the necessity with which it is
objectively represented cannot rest on any presupposition, as it does
with hypothetical imperatives. However, we should never lose sight of
the fact that whether there is any such categorical imperative cannot
be established by *example*, and hence empirically. For, we should
rather worry that everything that appears categorical may yet in some
hidden way be hypothetical. For example, when it is said that 'you
ought not to make deceitful promises', it is assumed that this necessity is not merely advice on how to avoid some other ill, as it would be
if it were said that 'you ought not to make lying promises, *because* if
they came to light your credibility would be ruined'. Rather, an action
of this kind must be considered as evil in itself, and thus the imperative
of prohibition is categorical. Therefore, no example can be put forward with certainty to show that the will is here determined merely
by the law and so without another drive, even if this is how things may
appear. For, it is always possible that the will may be influenced by
a secret fear of being shamed, or perhaps also a dark dread of other
dangers. Who can prove from experience that there is no such cause,
when all that it teaches is that we do not perceive one? If that were the
case then the so-called moral imperative, which appears categorical
and unconditional, would in fact be nothing more than a pragmatic
prescription, alerting us to our advantage and merely teaching us to
attend to it.

As a result, we will thus have to investigate the possibility of a *categorical* imperative in an entirely a priori manner, since we do not here

420 enjoy the advantage that its reality is shown by experience; if it were, we would only have to explain its possibility, not establish it. For now, however, this much is clear: that only the categorical imperative expresses a practical *law*, and that hypothetical imperatives can be called *principles* of the will, but not laws. This is because what it is *necessary* to do merely for attaining a purpose that happens to suit me can be regarded as *contingent*, and we can always be rid of the prescription if we give up the purpose. By contrast, the unconditional command of a categorical imperative leaves the will no free discretion to do otherwise, and hence alone carries with it that necessity which we require in a law.

Secondly, the reason why it is difficult to gain insight into the possibility of this categorical imperative or law of morality is a very serious one. It is an a priori synthetic practical proposition;[1]* and as it is so difficult to make sense of the possibility of such propositions when it comes to theoretical knowledge, it is plain that it will be no less difficult when it comes to practical knowledge.

Given this task, we can make a start by seeing whether perhaps the mere concept of a categorical imperative may perhaps provide us with the formula that contains the only proposition that can be a categorical imperative. For showing how such an absolute command is possible, even if we know what it asserts, must be deferred until the final section, as this will require special and arduous toil.

If I think in general terms about a *hypothetical* imperative, I do not know in advance what it will include, until its condition is specified. But when I think of a *categorical* imperative, I know straightaway what it includes. For beside the law, the imperative includes only the neces-

421 sity that the maxim[2] conform to this law, while the law includes no

---

¹ Without presupposing any inclination as its condition, I connect the action with the will a priori, and hence necessarily (though only objectively, i.e. under the idea of a reason that has complete control over all subjective motives). This is therefore a practical proposition that does not derive the willing of an action analytically from willing another that is already presupposed (for we have no such perfect will), but connects it immediately with the concept of the will of a rational being, though as something that is not contained in it.

² A *maxim* is the subjective principle for action, and must be distinguished from the *objective principle*, namely the practical law. The former contains the practical rule that reason determines in conformity with the conditions of the subject (quite often their ignorance, or their inclinations); it is thus the basis on which the subject *acts*. But the law

condition by which it is qualified. So nothing is left over with which the maxim of the action ought to conform except the universality of law as such; and it is only this conformity that the imperative actually represents as necessary.

Therefore there is just one categorical imperative, and it is this: *act only on a maxim that you can also* will to become a universal law.*

Now, if we can derive all imperatives of duty from this one imperative as their principle then, even though we cannot settle whether what gets called duty is an empty concept, we shall at least be able to indicate what we have in mind and what the concept involves.

Moreover, because the universality of laws governing effects constitutes what is properly called nature in the most general sense (as regards its form, i.e. the existence of things insofar as they are determined according to universal laws), the universal imperative of duty could also be expressed as follows: *act as if the maxim of your action, by your will, were to become a universal law of nature.*

We shall now enumerate some duties, dividing them in the usual way into duties to ourselves and to other human beings, and into perfect and imperfect duties.[1]

(1) A person who is reduced to hopelessness by a series of misfortunes feels weary of life, yet still possesses their reason and so can ask themselves whether it is not perhaps contrary to a duty to one's self to take one's own life. They now test to see whether the maxim of their action could possibly become a universal law of nature. But their maxim is: from self-love I make it my principle to shorten my life if, when protracted any longer, it threatens to make things worse for me rather than better. It only remains to be asked whether this principle of self-love could become a universal law of nature. But then one soon

422

---

is the objective principle, which is valid for every rational being, and is the basis on which they *ought to act*, i.e. an imperative.

[1] It should be noted that I completely postpone dealing with the division of duties until my future *Metaphysics of Morals*, and the one here is just put forward for the purpose of giving order to my examples. Furthermore, I here understand by a perfect duty one that never allows advantage to inclination to ground an exception,* so that among *perfect duties* I recognize those that are not only external but also internal. This goes against the way the word is used in schools, but I do not mean to argue for this here, since it does not matter for my purposes whether this point is conceded or not.

sees that any nature would contradict itself if its law were to destroy life by the very same feeling of self-love whose function it is to promote life; it could thus not subsist as nature. Hence that maxim could not possibly serve as a universal law of nature and is therefore completely contrary to the supreme principle of all duty.

(2) Out of need, another person finds themselves forced to borrow money. They know full well that they will not be able to repay it, but they also see that, unless they solemnly promise to repay it by a specified time, no one will lend them anything. They feel inclined to make such a promise; but they still have enough conscience to ask themselves: is it not impermissible and contrary to duty to escape need in this way? Suppose, however, they still decided to do this, then the maxim of their action would be as follows: when I think I need money I should borrow some and promise to repay it, even though I know I never will. This principle of self-love, or of personal advantage, is perhaps perfectly compatible with everything going well for me in the future; but the question is, is it right? I therefore transform this unreasonable demand of self-love into a universal law, and frame my question as follows: 'how would things stand if my maxim were to become a universal law?' I then see immediately that it could never hold as a universal law of nature and be consistent with itself, but rather must necessarily contradict itself. For if it became a universal law that anyone who believes themselves to be in need may promise whatever they like with the intention of not keeping it, then this would make the promise and the purpose one has in promising thereby impossible to achieve. For no one would believe they were being promised anything, but would laugh at any such utterance as a hollow pretence.

423 (3) A third person finds they have a talent that if cultivated could make them useful in all sorts of ways. But they are perfectly comfortable with their lot, and prefer to give themselves up to pleasure rather than to make the effort to expand and improve the aptitudes they are lucky enough to have been given by nature. Yet they still ask themselves: 'Does my maxim of neglecting my natural gifts agree, not merely with my tendency for indulgence, but also with what is called duty?' Now this person sees that nature could still continue under

such a universal law, even if human beings (like the South Sea Islanders) should let their talents rust and devote themselves merely to idleness, amusement, procreation—in a word, to enjoyment. Nonetheless, they cannot possibly *will* that this become a universal law of nature, or should be placed in us as such a law by natural instinct. For as a rational being they necessarily will that all their capacities are developed, because these capacities serve them and are given to them to be used in all sorts of ways.

(4) A fourth person is doing well, but sees that others whom they could easily help have to struggle with great hardships. They think: 'What's that to me? Let everyone be as happy as heaven intends, or as they can make themselves, I shall not take anything away from them or even envy them; but I don't feel inclined to contribute anything to their well-being, or help them in their condition of need!' Now, the human race could no doubt very well continue if such a way of thinking were to become a universal law of nature; indeed it could do so better than when everyone chatters about compassion and benevolence, and even occasionally develops the zeal to perform such actions, but at the same time cheats whenever they can by defrauding people of their rights or infringing them in some other way. But even though it is possible that a universal law of nature based on this maxim could very well obtain, it is still impossible to *will* that such a principle hold everywhere as a law of nature. For a will that resolved upon this would conflict with itself, as there can be many cases in which a person needs the love and compassion of others; but if their will were to give rise to a law of nature of this sort, they would rob themselves of all hope of the help they wish for.

   These, then, are some of the many actual duties—or which at least we take to be actual—and we can clearly see how to divide them up on the basis of the one principle stated above. We must *be able to will* that 424 a maxim of our action becomes a universal law: this is the general canon for morally judging our maxims. Some actions are such that their maxim cannot even be *thought* without contradiction, let alone that one could also will that it *should* become a law. There are other actions where there is no such inner impossibility, but it is still impossible to *will* that their maxim be dignified with the universality of a law of nature, because such a will would contradict itself. It is easy to see that actions of the first kind conflict with strict or narrower (inflexible) duty, while the second conflict only with wider (meritorious) duty.* Thus these examples have shown how all duties, as far as the kind of obligation is concerned (rather than the object of their action), can be set out completely in their dependence on the one principle.

If we think about what goes on in us whenever we transgress a duty, we find that we do not actually *will* that our maxim should become a universal law, since it is impossible for us to do so; rather, we will that the opposite of our maxim should stay in place as a general law, and instead take the liberty of making ourselves, or (again just this once) the gratification of our inclinations, an *exception* to it. Consequently, if we considered everything from one and the same point of view, namely that of reason, we would find a contradiction in our own will—namely, that a certain principle be objectively necessary as a universal law on the one hand, and yet on the other hand subjectively should not hold universally, but admit of exceptions. But there is no actual contradiction here, since we sometimes look at our actions from the point of view of a perfectly rational will, and sometimes look at just the same action also from the point of view of a will affected by inclination. Rather, what we have here is a resistance of inclination to the prescription of reason (*antagonismus*), by which the *universality* of the principle is transformed into something that has mere *general* validity; in this way, the practical rational principle is meant to meet the maxim halfway. Though our own judgement when used impartially cannot approve of this procedure, all this still proves that we do actually acknowledge the validity of the categorical imperative and permit ourselves (with all due respect for it) only a few exceptions that in our eyes are insignificant and forced upon us.

425   We have thus established at least this much: if duty is a concept that is to have meaning and actual legislative force over our actions, it can only be expressed in categorical imperatives, and certainly not hypothetical ones. Likewise (which is already a lot) we have put forward the content of the categorical imperative in a clear and useable way; and this imperative must contain the principle of all duty (if there is such a thing at all). But we have not yet got as far as proving

a priori that there actually is an imperative of this kind—that there is a practical law, which commands simply of itself without any further motivating drive, and that following this law is duty.

If we are to achieve this further goal, it is vital to heed this warning: forget any suggestion that the reality of this principle can be derived from some *particular property of human nature*. For duty has to be a practical, unconditional necessity of action; it must hold for all rational beings (to whom alone an imperative can apply), and *only in virtue of so holding* be a law also for every human will. This contrasts with whatever is derived from the distinctive natural disposition of human beings, from certain feelings and propensities, and indeed even (where possible) from a special tendency that is peculiar to human reason but which would not have to hold necessarily for the will of every rational being. Whatever is hereby derived can be a maxim for us, but not a law; it can give us a subjective principle on which propensity and inclination would have us act, but not an objective principle on which we would be *instructed* to act even if every propensity, inclination, and natural bent of ours were against it. Indeed, it proves the sublimity and inner dignity of the command of duty all the more, the less the subjective causes are in favour of it, and the more they are against it, without this weakening in the least the necessitation by the law, or taking anything away from its validity.

Here, then, we in fact see that philosophy finds itself in a precarious position; she is supposed to stand fast in spite of there being nothing in heaven from which she is suspended, or on earth by which she is supported. Here she is to prove her purity, as the authoress of her laws, rather than as the herald of those whispered to her by an innate sense, or by a tutelary nature of some kind. While laws of this latter sort may still be better than nothing at all, they can never be made   426 into principles dictated by reason. Such laws must have their source entirely a priori, and with it their commanding mien: to expect nothing from human inclination, but everything from the supremacy of the law and the respect it is owed, in failing which the human being is condemned to self-contempt and inner loathing.

Thus everything empirical is not only quite unfit to be added to the principle of morality; it is also highly prejudicial to the integrity of moral practices themselves. For in morality, the actual worth of an absolutely good will that is elevated above any price consists precisely in this: that the principle on which the will acts is free from all influences of contingent grounds, which is all that experience can provide. We cannot warn too strongly or too often against this slack or indeed base way of thinking, which seeks to identify this principle from among empirical motives and laws. For human reason in its weariness rests all too gladly on this cushion, and in a dream of sweet illusions (which lead it to embrace a cloud instead of Juno*) foists on morality a bastard patched from limbs of very diverse parentage, appearing in whatever way one wants, but not as Virtue does to whoever has beheld her in her true form.[1]

The question is therefore this: is it a necessary law *for all rational beings* always to judge their actions according to maxims which they themselves can will to serve as universal law? If so, then the law must already be bound up with the concept of the will of a rational being as such, in a completely a priori manner. But in order to uncover this connection one must, however reluctantly, take one step beyond, namely into metaphysics—albeit a region of metaphysics distinct from that of speculative philosophy, namely into the metaphysics of
427 morals. In a practical philosophy, our concern is not to engage with reasons for what *happens*, but rather with laws of what *ought to happen*, even if it never does, i.e. objective practical laws. And we do not need to investigate the reasons why something pleases or displeases; or how the pleasure of mere sensation differs from taste; or whether the latter differs from a universal delight of reason. Nor do we need to investigate the basis for the feeling of pleasure and displeasure, and how from these feelings there arise desires and inclinations, and maxims from them through co-operation with reason. For all of this belongs to empirical psychology, which would constitute the second part of the investigation of nature if one considers the latter as a *philosophy of nature*, insofar as it is founded on *empirical laws*. But what concerns us is the objective *practical* law, and hence the relation of a will to

---

[1] To behold Virtue in her real form is just to present morality stripped of any contamination by the sensuous and by any spurious adornment of reward or self-love. How much virtue then eclipses whatever appears enticing to the inclinations is something everyone can easily see who is willing to exert their reason in the slightest, if it has not been entirely spoilt for any form of abstract thinking.

itself, insofar as it determines itself merely through reason; as a result, everything that has reference to empirical matters falls away of itself. For, if *reason all by itself* determines conduct (and it is precisely this possibility that we now want to investigate), it must necessarily do this a priori.

The will is to be thought of as a capacity to determine itself in action *in conformity with the representation of certain laws*. And a capacity of this sort can only be found in rational beings. Now, what serves the will as the objective ground of its self-determination is the *end*; and this end, if it is given by reason alone, must be equally valid for all rational beings. By contrast, the *means* is merely that which makes an action possible, the effect of which is the end. The subjective ground of desire is the *drive*; the objective ground of willing is the *motivating reason*; hence the difference between subjective ends, which rest on drives, and objective ones, which depend on motivating grounds which hold for every rational being. Practical principles are *formal* if they abstract from all subjective ends; they are *material* if they have such ends, and hence certain drives, as their basis. Those ends that a rational being chooses for itself as *effects* of its actions (material ends) are all merely relative. This is because what gives them their worth is merely their relation to some particular faculty of desire, which cannot therefore provide any universal principles that are valid and necessary for all rational beings, or for all willing—that is, it can provide no practical laws. Thus all these relative ends are only the grounds of hypothetical imperatives. 428

But suppose there were something *the existence of which in itself* has an absolute worth, which then, as an *end in itself*, could be the ground of determinate laws: then the ground of a possible categorical imperative, i.e. of a practical law, would lie in this, and in this alone.

Now I say: a human being and generally every rational being *exists* as an end in itself, *not merely as a means* to be used at the pleasure of this or that will; rather, it must in all its actions, whether those are directed towards itself or also to other rational beings, always be considered *also as an end*. All the objects of inclination have only a conditional worth; for if the inclinations, and the needs founded on them, did not exist, their objects would have no worth. But the inclinations themselves, as sources of need, are so far from having an absolute worth that would make them desirable in their own right, that it must rather be the universal wish of every rational being to be entirely free from them. Therefore, the worth of an object *brought about* by our action is always conditional. Beings whose existence rests not on our will but on nature, if they are *non*-rational, still have only relative worth, as a means, and are therefore called *things*. On the other hand, *rational* beings are called *persons*, because their nature already marks them out as ends in themselves, i.e. as something that may not be used merely as a means; to that extent their nature limits all choice, and is an object of respect. Persons are therefore not merely subjective ends, the existence of which has a worth *for us* as the effect of our action. They are rather *objective ends*, i.e. entities whose existence in itself is an end, indeed such an end that no other end may be put in its place, to which they would *merely* serve as a means—for if this were not so, nothing of *absolute worth* could be found at all. But if all worth were conditional, and hence contingent, then no supreme practical principle for reason could be found at all either.

If, then, there is to be a supreme practical principle and, with regard to the human will, a categorical imperative, it must constitute 429 an objective principle of the will that can therefore serve as a universal practical law by virtue of representing what is, because an *end in itself*, necessarily an end for everyone. The basis of this principle is: *rational nature exists as an end in itself*. The human being necessarily represents their own existence this way; to that extent it is thus a *subjective* principle of human actions. But every other rational being also represents its existence in this way, on just the same rational ground that also holds for me.[1] It is thus at the same time an *objective* principle from which, as a supreme practical ground, it must be possible to derive all laws of the will. The practical imperative is thus the following: *Act in such a way that you treat humanity, whether in your own person or anyone else's, never merely as a means, but also always as an end.* Let us now see whether this derivation can be accomplished.

Keeping to the previous examples:

---

[1] I here put this proposition forward as a postulate. Its justification will be found in the final section.*

Firstly, regarding the concept of necessary duty to oneself, someone contemplating taking their own life asks themselves whether their action can be consistent with the idea of humanity *as an end in itself*. If they destroy themselves in order to escape from their burdens, they are making use of a person *merely as a means* to keep their life bearable up until its end. But the human being is not a thing, and hence is not something that can be treated *merely* as a means, but must in all of its actions* always be considered as an end in itself. Thus the human being in my own person is not at my disposal to be maimed, corrupted, or killed. (Here I must forgo the more precise account* of this principle which would be needed to avoid any misunderstandings: e.g. cases of limb amputation which are needed to save myself, or of endangering my life in order to preserve it, etc.; this task belongs to actual moral science.)

Secondly, regarding necessary or strict duty owed to others, a person who has it in mind to make a lying promise to others will see at once that they want to make use of another human being *merely as a means*, without the other sharing the end. For the person I want to use for my own purposes by such a promise cannot possibly agree to my way of behaving towards them and thus themselves share the end 430 of the action. This conflict with the principle of other human beings can be seen more clearly if one introduces examples of attacks on the freedom and property of others. For then it is clear that the one who violates the rights of human beings is disposed to make use of the person of others merely as a means, without taking into consideration that, as rational beings, they are always to be valued at the same time as ends, i.e. treated only as beings who must themselves be able to share in the end of the action in question.[1]

Thirdly, as regards contingent (meritorious) duties to oneself, it is not enough that the action does not conflict with humanity in our person, as an end in itself—it must also *harmonize with it*. Now it is

---

[1] Let no one think that here the trivial 'as you would not be treated yourself etc.' could serve as a guide or principle. For this is merely a derivation from our principle, with various limitations: it cannot be a universal law, as it does not contain the ground of duties to oneself; nor of duties of love to others (for many a person would happily agree that others should not benefit him, if only he might be exempt from showing them beneficence); nor of duties that are owed to one another, for the criminal would be able to argue on this basis against the judges who punish him, and so on.

part of nature's purpose for the humanity that lies in us as subjects that we have capacities for greater perfection. To neglect these capacities would perhaps be consistent with the *preservation* of humanity as an end in itself, but not with the *advancement* of this end.

Fourthly, as regards meritorious duty to others, the natural end that all human beings have is their happiness. Now the human race could indeed continue to exist even if, while not intentionally depriving others of their happiness, no one actively contributed anything to it. But unless everyone tries, as far as they can, to advance the ends of others, this is still only negatively and not positively in line with *humanity as an end in itself*. For if that notion is to have its *full* effect in me, the ends of a subject who is an end in themselves must, as much as possible, also be *my* ends.

This principle of humanity and of every rational nature as such, *as* 431 *an end in itself* (which is the supreme limiting condition of the freedom of action for every human being), is not borrowed from experience, for two reasons. First, because it is universal, as it concerns rational beings as such, and experience cannot tell us anything about that. Second, because in it humanity is not represented as a subjective end of human beings, i.e. as an object that one makes an end oneself, but as an objective end—an end that, as a law, is to constitute the supreme limiting condition on all subjective ends, whatever they happen to be. Hence, it must arise from pure reason. For in accordance with our first principle, the ground of all practical legislation lies *objectively in the rule* and the form of universality which makes it capable of being a law (or perhaps a law of nature). *Subjectively*, however, the ground of all practical legislation lies *in the end*. But in accordance with our second principle, the subject of all ends is every rational being, as an end in itself.

From this now follows the third practical principle of the will: the supreme condition of the will's harmony with universal practical reason is the idea of *the will of every rational being as a will that legislates universally*. According to this principle, all maxims are rejected which are not consistent with the will's own universal legislation. Thus the will is not just subject to the law, but subject to it in such a way that it must also be viewed as *self-legislating*—and only for this reason subject to the law (of which it can consider itself the author) in the first place.

The way we have been considering imperatives thus far—namely as actions conforming with law broadly similar to a *natural order*, or as the universal *supremacy as end* of rational beings in themselves—did manage to present their commanding mien without any mixture of interest as a driver, precisely because they were thought of as categorical. However, they were only *assumed* to be categorical, because this assumption was needed to explicate the concept of duty. That there *are* practical propositions that command categorically could not of itself be proved, any more than can be done in this section. One thing, however, might have been done: through some special feature it possesses, the imperative itself could indicate that interest has nothing to do with willing from duty, thereby distinguishing categorical from hypothetical imperatives. This is now achieved in the present third formulation of the principle, namely the idea of the will of every rational being as a *will that legislates universally*. 432

For, even though a will *that stands under laws* may still be bound to that law by means of some interest, nonetheless a will that is itself the supreme legislator cannot possibly, as such, depend on any interest. For a will that is dependent in this way would itself require yet another law to limit the interest of its self-love by the condition of being valid as a universal law.

Thus, if it is otherwise correct, the *principle* of every human will *as a will that legislates universally through all its maxims*[1] would be very well suited to be the categorical imperative. Because it involves the idea of universal legislation, it *is founded on no interest* and can thus alone, among all possible imperatives, be *unconditional*. Or better still, putting things the other way round: if there is a categorical imperative (i.e. a law for the will of every rational being), then the only command it can give is always to act on the maxim of a will whose object could at the same time be itself as legislating universally. For, only then is the practical principle, and the imperative the will obeys, unconditional, because it cannot be based on any interest whatsoever.

Now, if we look back at all previous efforts that have ever been made to discover the principle of morality, it is no wonder that they

---

[1] I can here be excused from providing examples to illustrate this principle, since those that first illustrated the categorical imperative and its formula can all serve the same purpose here.

were destined to come to nothing. It was recognized that human beings are bound to laws by their duty, but it did not occur to anyone that human beings are subject to a legislation that is *only their own*, but is for all that also *universal*; and so are only obligated to act in conformity with a will which is their own, but which, in accordance with nature's purposes, legislates universally. For, by thinking of human beings as subject to a law (whatever it may be), it was supposed that this law had 433 to carry with it some interest as enticement or constraint, because it did not arise as a law from *their own* will; the will was instead necessitated by *something else* to act in a certain way, in mere conformity with a law. With this inevitable conclusion, however, all the labour that had gone into trying to find a supreme ground of duty was irretrievably squandered. For duty was missed, and what one got instead was just the necessity of an action from a certain interest, be it one's own or that of another. But then the imperative always had to turn out to be a conditional one, and not fit to be a moral command at all. I shall therefore call my basic position the principle of the *autonomy* of the will, in opposition to all others, which I accordingly count as *heteronomy*.

This concept of every rational being—beings who have to consider themselves as legislating universally through the maxim of their will in order to judge themselves and their actions from this universal point of view—leads to a very fruitful concept that is closely connected with it: namely, that of *a kingdom* of ends*.

I understand by *kingdom* here the systematic union of various rational beings through common laws. Now, laws determine ends according to their validity for all universally. One can therefore (if one abstracts from the personal differences among rational beings, and likewise from all content of their private ends) conceive of a systematically connected whole of all ends (of rational beings as ends in themselves, as well as the ends that each of them may set for themselves), i.e. a kingdom of ends, which, according to the principles given above, is possible.

For, as we have seen, all rational beings stand under the *law* that each of them is to treat themselves and all others *never merely as a means*, but always *at the same time as ends in themselves*. But by this there arises a systematic union of rational beings through common objective laws—i.e. a kingdom. And because the purpose of these laws is precisely to connect these beings to one another as ends and means, it can be called a kingdom of ends (though admittedly only as an ideal).

A rational being, however, belongs to the kingdom of ends as a *member* if they legislate universally in the kingdom but are also subject to these laws. They belong to it *as sovereign* if as legislating they are not subject to the will of another.

A rational being must always regard themselves as lawgiving 434 (whether as a member or as its sovereign) in a kingdom of ends which is made possible through freedom of the will. But they cannot maintain the position of sovereign merely through the maxims of their will, but only if they are a completely independent being, without any needs or any limitations on their capacity to carry out their will.

Thus morality consists in referring all action to the legislation that is required to make possible a kingdom of ends. But this lawgiving must be found in every rational being themselves and must be capable of arising from the will of that being. The principle of their will is therefore this: never to perform any action except one whose maxim could be a universal law, and thus to act only on a maxim *through which the will could regard itself at the same time as enacting universal law*. Now, if maxims are not already by their nature in accord with this objective principle of rational beings as universally legislating, then the necessity of an action in accordance with this principle is called practical necessitation, i.e. *a duty*. Duty does not apply to the sovereign in the kingdom of ends, but it does to every member of it, and indeed to all to the same degree.

The practical necessity of acting in accordance with this principle, i.e. duty, therefore does not rest at all on feelings, impulses, or inclinations. Rather, it merely rests on the relation of rational beings to one another, a relation in which the will of a rational being must always be regarded as *lawgiving*, because otherwise they could not be thought of as *ends in themselves*. Thus for every maxim of a universally legislating will, reason makes reference to every other will and also to every action directed towards itself. It does so not to give itself any additional practical motivating ground or future advantage, but from the idea of the *dignity* of a rational being that obeys no law other than that which they also give themselves.

In the kingdom of ends, everything has either a *price* or *dignity*. What has a *price* can be replaced with something else, as its *equivalent*. By contrast, whatever is exalted above all price and hence admits of no equivalent has *dignity*.

Whatever relates to general human inclinations and needs has a *market price*. Whatever, irrespective of any such need, is nonetheless in conformity with a certain taste, that is, delight in the purposeless 435 play of the powers of our mind,* has an *aesthetic price*.* But what constitutes the condition under which alone something can be an end in itself does not merely have a relative worth or price; rather, it has an inner worth, or *dignity*.

Now morality is the only condition under which a rational being can be an end in itself, because it is only through this that it is possible to be a legislating member of the kingdom of ends. Thus morality, and humanity insofar as it is capable of morality, is the only thing that has dignity. Skill and hard work have a market price; wit, lively imagination, and humour have an aesthetic price. By contrast, promise-keeping and acting benevolently from principles (rather than from instinct) have an inner worth. If these are lacking, neither nature nor art contain anything that can replace them; for their worth does not consist in their effects, or in the advantage or utility they produce, but in the dispositions—that is, the maxims of the will—which in this way are ready to be revealed in actions, even if they are not favoured by success. Moreover, these actions need no recommendation from any subjective proclivity, taste, no immediate propensity or feeling, to look upon them with immediate favour or delight. For they represent the will that performs such actions as the object of an immediate respect, as nothing but reason is required to *impose* these actions on the will—rather than *wheedling* them out of the will, which in the case of duties would be a contradiction anyway. Our appraisal thus reveals that the worth such a mode of thinking has is dignity; this puts it infinitely above any price, so that it cannot be weighed or compared against anything else without thereby violating its sanctity, as it were.

And what is it, then, that entitles a morally good disposition or virtue to make such lofty claims? It is nothing less than the *share* it secures for a rational being *in universal legislation*, which makes it fit to be a member of a possible kingdom of ends. It was already marked out for this by its own nature as an end in itself, and thus as legislating in the kingdom of ends; as free with regards to all laws of nature, obeying only those laws that it gives itself and according to which its maxims can belong to a universal legislation (to which it also subjects 436 itself). For nothing has any worth other than a worth determined for it by the law. But precisely because of this, the legislation that determines all worth must have a dignity, i.e. an unconditional and incomparable worth, for which the word *respect* is the only suitable expression for the esteem that a rational being is to give it. *Autonomy* is thus the ground of the dignity of human nature, and of every rational nature.

The three ways of representing the principle of morality given above are fundamentally just so many formulations of precisely the same law, one of which of itself unites the other two within it. However, there is still a difference between them, which is more subjectively than objectively practical: that is to say, the way in which they bring an idea of reason closer to intuition (through a certain analogy) and thereby to feeling. For all maxims have:

1. a *form*, which consists in universality, and then the moral imperative is formulated as follows: 'maxims must be chosen as if they were to hold as universal laws of nature';
2. a *matter*, namely an end, and then the formula says, 'for every maxim, a rational being, which by its nature is an end, and hence an end in itself, must serve as the limiting condition of all merely relative and arbitrarily chosen ends';
3. a *complete determination* of all maxims by means of the following formula: 'that all maxims arising from one's own lawgiving are to harmonize into a possible kingdom of ends as a kingdom of nature'.[1]

---

[1] Teleology considers nature as a kingdom of ends; moral theory considers a possible kingdom of ends as a kingdom of nature. In the former, the kingdom of ends is a theoretical idea for explaining what exists. In the latter, it is a practical idea, aiming to bring about that which does not exist, but which could become actual through our conduct, if it were carried out in conformity with this idea.

The development here is, as it were, through the category of the *unity* of the form of the will (its universality), to the *plurality* of the matter (of objects, i.e. of ends), to their systematic *togetherness* or totality. However, in making moral *judgements*, it is always better to proceed by the strict method and to take as one's basic principle the universal formulation of the categorical imperative: *act in accordance*
437 *with the maxim that can also be made a universal law*. Nonetheless, if one also wants to make the moral law accessible, it helps a great deal to bring one and the same action under the said three categories and thereby, as far as is possible, bring it closer to intuition.

We can now conclude with the point from which we began, namely with the concept of an unconditionally good will. A *will is absolutely good* that cannot be evil, hence whose maxim, if it is made into a universal law, can never conflict with itself. This principle is therefore also the supreme law of such a will: always act on that maxim which you can also will to be universal as a law. This is the only condition under which a will can never be in conflict with itself, and such an imperative is categorical. Moreover, the validity of the will, as a universal law for possible actions, is analogous with the universal connection of the existence of things according to universal laws, which is what the formal in nature consists in. The categorical imperative can thus also be expressed as follows: *act in accordance with maxims that can also have themselves as their object as universal laws of nature.* This, then, is the formula of an absolutely good will.

A rational nature distinguishes itself from other natures by setting itself an end. This end would be the matter of every good will. But, in the idea of a will absolutely good without any qualification (i.e. regardless of whether it attains this or that end), one must abstract altogether from every end that has to be *actually brought about* (as this would make every will only relatively good). Therefore, the end in question must be thought of not as an end to be actually brought about, *but as a self-sufficient end*, conceived only negatively, as that which no action may contravene, and which must in all our willing therefore never be valued merely as a means, but always also as an end. Now this end can be nothing other than the subject of all possible ends, because it is also the subject of a possible absolutely good will; for it cannot, without contradiction, be ranked lower than any other object. Accordingly, these two principles are, at bottom, the same: 'so act with reference to every rational being (both yourself and others) that in your maxim it counts also as an end in itself', and 'act on a maxim that also contains in itself its own universal validity for every 438 rational being'. For to say that in using the means to an end, my maxim ought to be qualified by the condition that it should also be universally valid as a law for every subject, is tantamount to saying that the subject of ends, i.e. the rational being itself, must be made the foundation of all maxims of actions and never merely a means—instead it must be the supreme condition limiting the use of all means, and hence always at the same time an end.

From this it unquestionably follows that every rational being, as an end in itself, must be able to view itself as also legislating universally with regard to any law whatever to which it may be subject. For, it is precisely this fittingness of its maxims for universal legislation that marks it out as an end in itself. Likewise, this dignity (prerogative) which it has above all merely natural beings carries with it the necessity of always choosing its maxims not just from its own point of view, but also from that of all other rational beings as legislators (who are therefore also called 'persons'). Now in this way a world of rational beings (an intelligible world) as a kingdom of ends is possible, and possible through the legislation of all persons themselves as members. Accordingly, every rational being must so act as if through its maxims it were at all times a legislating member of the universal kingdom of ends. The formal principle of these maxims is: so act as if your maxim were to serve at the same time as a universal law (of all rational beings). Thus a kingdom of ends is only possible in an analogous way to a kingdom of nature; however, the former is possible only through maxims, i.e. self-imposed rules; the latter only through laws of externally necessitated efficient causes. In spite of this difference, we give nature as a whole, even though it is regarded as a machine, the name of a 'kingdom of nature' insofar as and because it has a relation to rational beings as its ends.

Now a kingdom of ends would actually come into being through maxims the rule of which the categorical imperative prescribes to all rational beings—*if they were universally followed*. But a rational being that himself were to follow this maxim punctiliously cannot count on

everyone else being true to it as well; nor can he count on the kingdom of nature and its purposes harmonizing with him, as a worthy mem-
439 ber, into a kingdom of ends that he makes possible, i.e. that the kingdom of nature will favour his expectations for happiness. Despite this, the law 'act according to the maxims of a member legislating universally for a merely possible kingdom of ends' remains in full force because it commands categorically. And in this lies the paradox: that the mere dignity of humanity, as rational nature, without any other end or advantage to be obtained by it, and hence out of respect for a mere idea, is still to serve as an unrelenting prescription of the will. Moreover, it is just in this independence of a maxim from all such drives that the sublimity of rational nature consists, and the worthiness of every rational subject to be a legislating member in the kingdom of ends—for otherwise they would have to be viewed only as subject to the natural law of their needs. Even if both the natural kingdom and the kingdom of ends were thought of as united under one sovereign, so that the latter would no longer remain a mere idea but obtain true reality, rational nature would thereby doubtless gain an additional strong drive, but it would not undergo any increase in inner worth. For, despite this, even this sole unconstrained legislator would still have to be thought of as judging the worth of rational beings only by their disinterested conduct, prescribed to them directly, merely from that idea. The essence of things is not altered by their external relations; and what constitutes the absolute worth of a human being alone, disregarding these relations, is that by which they must be judged—by anyone whatsoever, even by the supreme being. *Morality* is thus the relation of actions to the autonomy of the will—that is, to a possible universal legislation through its maxims. An action that can be consistent with the autonomy of the will is *permissible*; one that does not agree with this is *impermissible*. A will whose maxims necessarily harmonize with the laws of autonomy is a *holy*, absolutely good will. The dependence of a will that is not absolutely good on the principle of autonomy (i.e. moral necessitation) is *obligation*. Obligation therefore cannot apply to a holy being. The objective necessity of an action from obligation is called *duty*.

From what has just been said, it can now easily be explained how we think of the concept of duty in terms of subjection to the law, and

yet at the same time see a certain sublimity and *dignity* in the person 440
who fulfils all their duties. For while there is indeed no sublimity in
being *subject* to the moral law, there is insofar as one is also its *legislator*, and only because of that subordinated to it. Also, we have shown
above that neither fear, nor inclination, but only respect for the law is
the drive that can give an action a moral worth. Our own will is the
proper object of respect insofar as it acts under the condition of
a possible universal legislation through its maxims (which is possible
for us as an idea), and the dignity of humanity consists precisely in
this capacity to legislate universally, although with the qualification of
also being itself subject to this same legislation.

The autonomy of the will as the supreme principle of morality

Autonomy of the will is the property through which the will is a law
to itself (independently of any property of the objects of willing). The
principle of autonomy is thus: not to choose except in such a way that
the maxims of one's choice are also included as universal law in the
same act of willing. Because it is a synthetic proposition, it cannot be
proved by mere analysis of the concepts that occur in it that this
practical rule is an imperative, i.e. that the will of every rational being
is necessarily bound to the rule as a condition. To prove it one would
have to go beyond knowledge of objects and move into a critique
of the subject, i.e. of pure practical reason, since this synthetic
proposition, which commands apodictically, must be capable of being
known completely a priori. However, this is not the business of the
present section.* But that the aforesaid principle of autonomy is the
sole principle of moral science can be established perfectly well by
mere analysis of the concepts of morality. For analysis shows us that
the principle of morality must be a categorical imperative, and that
what it commands is neither more nor less than this autonomy.

The heteronomy of the will as the source of all 441
spurious principles of morality

If the will seeks the law that is to determine it in *anything other* than
the fitness of its maxims for its own universal legislation, and hence if

it thereby goes outside itself in seeking for the law in a property of any of its objects, the outcome is always *heteronomy*. Then the will does not give itself the law, but rather the object does so through its relation to the will. Whether it rests on inclination, or on representations of reason, it is only hypothetical imperatives that are made possible by this relation: I ought to do something *because I want something else*. By contrast, the moral and hence categorical imperative says: I ought to act in such or such a way, even if I do not want anything else. For example, the hypothetical imperative says: 'I ought not to lie if I want to retain my honourable reputation'. But the categorical imperative says: 'I ought not to lie, even if it did not bring me the slightest disgrace'. The latter imperative must therefore abstract from all objects to the extent that they have no *influence* at all on the will; thus practical reason (the will) does not merely administer an interest that is alien to it, but instead thereby demonstrates its own commanding mien, as supreme legislation. So for example I ought to try to advance a happiness which is not my own, not because the realization of that happiness is of consequence to me (whether because of some immediate inclination or some delight gained indirectly through reason), but merely because the maxim that excludes it cannot be comprised in one and the same willing, as universal law.

Classification of all possible principles of morality based on heteronomy as their assumed fundamental concept

Human reason has here tried every possible wrong route before successfully hitting on the only true one—as it always does in its pure use, until it has been subjected to critique.*

All principles that can be entertained from the point of view of heteronomy are either *empirical* or *rational*. Principles of the *first* kind, based on the principle of *happiness*, are built on physical or moral feeling. Principles of the *second* kind, based on the principle of *perfection*, are built on the rational concept of a perfection which is either a possible effect of our will, or an independently existing perfection (namely God's will), as a determining cause of our will.*

Empirical principles are not fit to be the foundation of moral laws at all. For the universality with which such laws must hold for all rational beings without any distinction, and the unconditional practical necessity that is thereby imposed on them, disappears if their ground is taken from the *particular arrangement of human nature*, or the accidental circumstances in which it is placed. Yet the most objectionable is the principle of *one's own happiness*. This is not just because it is false, and experience contradicts the supposition that well-being and acting well always coincide; nor merely because it contributes nothing whatsoever to the grounding of morality, since making a human being happy is quite different from making them good, and making them prudent and wise with regard to their own advantage is quite different from making them virtuous. Rather, what makes this view truly objectionable is that it bases morality on drives, which undermine it and destroy its sublimity, putting virtuous and vicious motives in the same class and only teaching us to become better at calculating, while obliterating the specific difference between the two. By contrast, the supposed special sense of moral feeling[1] remains closer to morality and its dignity (however shallow it is to appeal to it, as do those who are unable to *think* but believe they can help themselves out by *feeling*, even when nothing except universal laws will do: for feelings, which by nature differ infinitely in degree from one another, cannot offer a uniform measure of good and evil; and one can in no way make a valid judgement for others through one's feelings). This position at least does Virtue the honour of attributing to her *immediately* the delight and high esteem we have for her, and does not, as it were, tell 443 her to her face that we are attached to her not for her beauty, but only for our own advantage.

Among the *rational* or reason-based grounds of morality, the ontological concept of *perfection* is nevertheless better than the theological concept that derives morality from the divine and supremely perfect will (however empty, indeterminate, and hence useless it is for finding, in the immense sum of possible reality, the greatest sum that is

[1] The reason why I classify the principle of moral feeling along with that of happiness is that every empirical interest promises to contribute to our well-being by the agreeableness that something has to offer, whether this happens immediately and without a view to any advantages, or with regard to those advantages. Likewise, one must, with *Hutcheson*, classify the principle of sharing in the happiness of others with the moral sense which he proposed.

proper for us; and however much, in trying specifically to distinguish the reality that is here in question from every other, it cannot avoid going round in a circle, and surreptitiously presupposing the morality it is supposed to explain). It is better not only because we cannot intuit the perfection of a divine will and so can derive it only from our concepts, the foremost of which is morality; but even worse, if we try to avoid going round in such a crude explanatory circle (and so do *not* derive the perfection of the divine will from morality), then the only concept of this will that we would have left would have to be the foundation for a system of morals directly opposed to morality—as our concept of this divine will could then only be made up of attributes such as the desire for honour and domination, combined with terrifying ideas of power and the zeal for vengeance.

But if I had to choose between the concept of moral sense and that of perfection as such (which at least do not infringe on morality, even though both are quite unfit to support it as its foundation), I would opt for the latter. For at least it transfers the decision of the question from sensibility to the judicial court of pure reason—even if it decides nothing there—thereby preserving the indeterminate idea of a will good in itself without distorting it, and leaving it open for further determination.

Beyond this, I believe I may be exempt from a lengthy refutation of all these doctrines. This could be done so easily, and presumably be so well understood even by those whose office requires them to declare themselves for one or other of these theories (because their audience will not allow them to sit on the fence), that to spend time on it would be merely superfluous labour. But what is of more interest here is to know that these principles set up nothing other than heteronomy as the primary ground of morality, and precisely because of this must necessarily fall short of their goal.

444   Whenever an object of the will has to be made the foundation for prescribing the rule that determines the will, the rule is nothing other than heteronomy. The imperative is then conditional: '*if* or *because* one wills this object, one ought to act in such or such a way'. Hence it can never command morally, i.e. categorically. The object may determine the will by means of inclination, as with the principle of one's own happiness; or by means of reason directed to objects of our

possible willing as such, in the case of the principle of perfection. Either way, the will never determines itself *immediately*, by the representation of the action, but only by a drive that the anticipated effect of the action brings to bear on the will: *I ought to do something because I want something else*. And here yet another law in me as a subject, according to which I necessarily will this something else, must be made the foundation; and *this* law in turn requires an imperative to limit this maxim. Because the representation of an object to be attained by our own powers gives rise, in accordance with the natural constitution of the subject, to an impulse exercised on its will, an impulse which belongs to the nature of the subject (whether to sensibility—to inclination or taste—or to understanding and reason, which by the special arrangement of their nature take delight in being exercised on an object), it would actually be nature which gives the law. As a result, this law must not only be known and proved by experience, and hence be in itself contingent and unfit to be an apodictic practical rule, which morality requires; it is also *always only heteronomy* of the will—the will does not give the law to itself, but an alien impulse gives it to it, by means of the susceptibility of a subject whose nature is so attuned.

An absolutely good will, whose principle must be a categorical imperative, will therefore be indeterminate with regard to all objects, and contain only the *form of willing* as such, and that form is autonomy. That is, the suitability of the maxim of every good will to make itself into a universal law is the only law which the will of every rational being imposes on itself, without underpinning the law with any drive or interest as its foundation.

How such a synthetic a priori practical proposition is possible and why it is necessary is a problem that cannot be resolved within the bounds of the metaphysics of morals; nor have we asserted its truth here, much less pretended that it is within our power to give a proof. By 445 unpacking the generally held concept of morality, we have merely shown that an autonomy of the will unavoidably attaches to it, or rather lies at its foundation. Whoever takes morality to be something, and not a chimerical idea without truth, must therefore also concede its principle stated above. Thus, like the first section, this one was also analytic. However, that morality is no phantasm—a conclusion which follows if the categorical imperative and with it the autonomy of the will is true, and absolutely necessary as an a priori principle—requires a *possible synthetic use of pure practical reason*. But we cannot venture on such a use without a prior *critique* of this rational faculty itself. In our final section, we shall outline the principal features of this faculty, as far as is required for our purposes.

SECTION III

TRANSITION FROM THE METAPHYSICS OF MORALS TO THE CRITIQUE OF PURE PRACTICAL REASON

The concept of freedom is the key to explaining the autonomy of the will

The *will* is a kind of causality that living beings have insofar as they are rational. *Freedom* would then be a property of this causality insofar as the will is capable of acting independently of any alien causes *determining* it; while *natural necessity* is the property that characterizes the causality of all non-rational beings—namely the property of being determined into activity by the influence of alien causes.

This characterization of freedom is *negative* and therefore unfruitful in gaining insight into its essence; but a *positive* concept of freedom flows from it which is so much the richer and more fruitful. The concept of causality carries with it that of *laws*, according to which, when we call something a cause, something else must be supposed, namely the effect. Likewise freedom, although it is not a property the will has by virtue of natural laws, is not thereby completely lawless. Freedom must rather be a causality in accordance with immutable laws, but of a special kind; for otherwise a free will would be an absurdity. As we have seen, natural necessity is a heteronomy of efficient causes, for every effect can only come about in accordance with the law that something else determines the efficient cause. What else, then, can freedom of the will be, other than autonomy—that is, the property the will has of being a law to itself? But the proposition 'the will is in all its actions a law to itself' just signifies the principle of acting on no maxim except that which can also have itself as its object as a universal law. And this is precisely the formula of the categorical imperative and the principle of morality: thus a free will and a will under moral laws are one and the same.

Thus, if freedom of the will is presupposed, morality along with its principle follows from it, by mere analysis of its concept. Nonetheless the latter is always a synthetic proposition,* namely that an absolutely good will is that whose maxim, when considered as a universal law, can always be contained within itself. For that property of its maxim cannot be discovered by analysis of the concept of an absolutely good will. The only thing that makes synthetic propositions of this sort possible is if two cognitions are bound together by their connection with a third thing in which they are both to be found. This third thing is supplied by the *positive* concept of freedom, and cannot be nature as the sensible world (in the concept of which the concepts of something as the cause in relation to *something else* as the effect come together, and which is therefore the third thing with respect to physical causes). What this third thing is to which freedom points us, and of which we have an idea a priori, cannot be stated here straightaway; nor can we make comprehensible the deduction of the concept of freedom from pure practical reason, and with it the possibility of a categorical imperative. All this requires some further preparation.

Freedom must be presupposed as a property of the will of all rational beings

It is not enough to ascribe freedom to our will on whatever grounds, unless we have sufficient grounds to attribute it to all rational beings as well. For morality serves as a law for us only insofar as we are *rational beings*; it must therefore hold for all rational beings as well. Moreover, since it must be derived solely from the property of freedom, freedom must also be shown to be a property of the will of all rational beings. And it is not enough to establish this freedom from certain alleged experiences of human nature (although it is actually absolutely impossible to do so, as this can only be established a priori); rather, freedom must be shown to belong to the activity of rational beings endowed with a will as such. I say: every being who cannot act except *under the idea of freedom* is precisely because of that actually free in a practical respect; that is, all laws that are inseparably bound up with freedom hold for it just as if its will had also been pronounced free in itself in a way that is valid in theoretical philosophy.[1] I now assert: to every rational being that has a will, we must necessarily grant the idea of freedom under which alone it acts. For we think of such a being as having a reason that is practical, i.e. that has causality in regard to its objects. Now, it is impossible to think of a reason that would self-consciously receive guidance from elsewhere with regard to its judgements, since the subject would then not attribute the determination of judgement to their reason, but to an impulse. Reason must regard itself as the author of its own principles, independently of an alien influence. Consequently, as practical reason, or as the will of a rational being, it must view itself as free. That is, its will can be a will of its own only under the idea of freedom, and must for practical purposes be ascribed to all rational beings.

Of the interest that attaches to the ideas of morality

We have finally traced the determinate concept of morality back to the idea of freedom. But we could not demonstrate this freedom as something actual, even in ourselves and in human nature: we only saw that we must presuppose it if we are to think of a being as rational and endowed with a consciousness of its own causality with regard to its actions, i.e. endowed with a will. And we find that on just the same grounds, we must ascribe this property of self-determining action under the idea of freedom to every being endowed with reason and will.

But from the presupposition of these ideas, there also flowed the consciousness of a law for acting, namely: that the subjective principles of actions, i.e. maxims, must always be so taken that they can also hold objectively, i.e. universally as principles, and hence serve for our own universal legislation. But why should I subject myself to this principle, and do so as a rational being as such, and in so doing also subject to it every other being endowed with reason? I am willing to concede that

449

---

[1] This approach takes it as sufficient for our purpose if freedom is presupposed merely as an *idea* by all rational beings as foundational to their actions; and I adopt it in order not to incur the obligation of proving freedom from a theoretical point of view as well. For even if this latter point is left unresolved, the same laws that would bind a being that was actually free still hold for a being that cannot act except under the idea of its own freedom. In this way we can liberate ourselves from the burden that weighs upon the theoretical approach.

no interest *impels* me to do this, since that would provide no categorical imperative; but I must still necessarily *take* an interest in it, and see how this can be the case. For this 'I ought' is actually an 'I will'* that holds for every rational being, provided that its practical reason is without any hindrances; but for beings like us—who are also affected by drives of a different kind, stemming from sensibility, and for whom what reason would do is not always what is actually done—that necessity of action is only called an 'ought', and the subjective necessity is distinguished from the objective one.

It therefore appears that in the idea of freedom we actually just presupposed the moral law, namely the principle of the autonomy of the will itself, without being able to prove its reality and objective necessity as such. Even this much would have been a considerable achievement, because we would at least have determined the genuine principle of morality more accurately than has been done previously. Nonetheless, we would have made no progress regarding establishing the principle's validity, and the practical necessity of subjecting oneself to it. For we would still not be able to give a satisfactory answer if someone were to ask us these fundamental questions: Why must the universal validity of our maxim as a law be the condition which restricts our actions? What is the basis for the worth we ascribe to this way of acting, which is so great that there can be no higher interest of any kind? And how can it be that a human being feels that their per-
450 sonal worth comes through this alone, compared to which the worth of a pleasant or unpleasant state is to be taken as nothing?

It is indeed possible for us to take an interest in aspects of our character, where this interest is not in being in any particular state, but rather in the fact that those aspects of our character would qualify us to partake in that state if it were to be apportioned by reason. That is to say, the mere worthiness to be happy can interest us of itself, even without the motivating ground of partaking in this happiness; but this judgement is in fact only the effect of already presupposing the importance of moral laws (when by means of the idea of freedom, we detach ourselves from every empirical interest). But that we ought to detach ourselves from such empirical interests is something we cannot yet see; so we cannot yet see why we ought to consider ourselves as free in acting, yet subject to certain laws, and thereby find in our own person a worth that can compensate for the loss of everything else that has worth for us. How this is possible, and hence *how the moral law can be binding*, is something we do not yet see.

One must frankly admit that a kind of circle appears here, from which it seems there is no escape. On the one hand, we take ourselves to be free in the order of efficient causes in order to think ourselves under moral laws in the order of ends; on the other hand, we think of ourselves as subject to these laws because we have ascribed to ourselves freedom of the will—for freedom and the will's own legislation are both autonomy, and hence equivalent concepts.* However, precisely because of this, one of them cannot be used to explicate the other or specify its grounds. This equivalence can at most be used for the logical purposes of reducing seemingly different representations of the same object to a single concept (in the way that different fractions of the same value can be reduced to their lowest common denominator).

And yet an escape route still remains open for us: namely to consider whether we take up one standpoint when, through freedom, we think of ourselves as a priori efficient causes, and another standpoint when we represent ourselves based on our actions as effects that we see before our eyes.

There is one point which requires no subtle thinking, and which one can assume even the commonest understanding can grasp (though no doubt in its own way, through an obscure sense of a distinction made by the power of judgement, and which that common understanding calls 'feeling'). This point is as follows: all representations that come to us involuntarily (like those of the senses) enable us to know objects as they affect us, while what they may be in themselves remains unknown to us. Hence, as far as representations of this kind are concerned, even if the understanding makes every effort to be attentive and clear-sighted, we can only achieve knowledge of *appearances*, never of *things in themselves*.* Once this distinction is drawn (perhaps just by noting the difference between ideas given to us passively from without, and ideas which we actively produce from ourselves), it follows directly that behind appearances we must allow and assume something else which is not appearance—namely things in themselves. And since we can never be acquainted with the latter,

451

but only with the way in which they affect us, we must resign ourselves to being unable to get any closer to them, or ever knowing what
they are in themselves. This must give rise to a distinction, however
crude, between a *world of sense* and the *world of understanding*. The
first of these can vary a great deal because of differences in the
sensibility of the many kinds of observers in the world, while the second, which is its foundation, always remains the same. Even as
regards their own self, a human being cannot presume to know how it
is in itself, based on the acquaintance they have with themselves in
inner sensation. For since they do not as it were create themselves,
and since they acquire their concept of themselves not a priori but
empirically, it is natural that they can only come to know about themselves through inner sense, and thus only through the way their
nature appears and the way their consciousness is affected. But they
necessarily assume that there is something beyond these characteris-
tics of their own subject that are composed of nothing but appearances, which lies at their foundation: namely its 'I', such as it may be
in itself. Thus with respect to mere perception and receptivity to sensations the subject must count themselves as belonging to the *world of
sense*; but as regards what there may be of pure activity in them (that
which reaches consciousness, not by affecting the senses, but immediately), the subject must count themselves as belonging to the *intellectual world*, though of that world they know nothing more.

452   A reflective human being must reach a conclusion of this sort
about all the things that may present themselves to them. Presumably
it is also to be found in the commonest understanding, which is
known to be much inclined to expect that behind the objects of the
senses there is something invisible, and active in its own right. But
then it spoils matters by making this invisible thing sensuous again,
wanting to make it an object of intuition, and thereby ending up none
the wiser.

Now, a human being actually finds in themselves a capacity which
distinguishes them from all other things, and even from their own self
insofar as it is affected by objects, and that is *reason*. As pure self-
generated activity, it is elevated even above the *understanding* in this
respect.* The latter also involves self-generated activity, and so unlike
the senses does not merely comprise representations generated when

one is passively affected by things. Nevertheless, the activity of the understanding can only produce concepts that *bring sensuous representations under rules* and thereby unite them in one consciousness; without using sensibility it could think nothing at all. By contrast, reason, when it comes to *ideas,** shows a spontaneity so pure that it goes beyond anything that is given by sensibility, while its highest vocation is manifested in distinguishing the world of sense from the world of understanding, and thereby marking out for the understanding its own limits.

On account of this, a rational being must view itself qua *intelligence* (rather than from the side of its lower powers) as not belonging to the world of sense, but to that of the understanding. It thus has two standpoints from which it can consider itself, and recognize laws for the use of its powers, and consequently for all its actions: *first* as under laws of nature (heteronomy) insofar as it belongs to the world of sense; and *secondly*, insofar as it belongs to the intelligible world, under laws that are independent of nature and not empirical, but have their foundation merely in reason.

As a rational being, and hence as one that belongs to the intelligible world, a human being can never think of the causality of their own will except under the idea of freedom; for freedom *just is* being independent from the determining causes of the sensible world, and this independence is what reason must always ascribe to itself. Now, the idea of freedom is inseparably connected to the concept of *autonomy*, and then with this the universal principle of morality, which, as that idea, lies at the foundation of all actions of *rational* beings, just as the   453 law of nature lies at the foundation of all appearances.

We have now removed the suspicion which we voiced earlier, namely that there might be a hidden circle in our reasoning from freedom to autonomy and from autonomy to the moral law. The suspicion was that perhaps we were presupposing the idea of freedom only for the sake of the moral law, in order subsequently to derive the moral law from freedom. This would have meant we were unable to ground freedom, but only assume it by pleading for a principle which right-minded souls would gladly concede us, but which we could never establish as a demonstrable proposition. For now we see that, when we think of ourselves as free, we transfer ourselves into the world of understanding as members, and acknowledge the autonomy of the will along with its consequence, morality; but if we think of duty as something that binds us, we consider ourselves both as belonging to the world of sense and yet at the same time to the world of the understanding.

How is a categorical imperative possible?

As an intelligence, a rational being counts itself as belonging to the world of understanding, while simply as an efficient cause belonging to that world, it calls its causality a *will*. But viewed from the other side, it is also conscious of itself as a part of the world of sense, in which its actions are encountered as mere appearances of that causality. However, we cannot grasp how these actions are possible through the causality of the will, since we have no acquaintance with this causality. Rather, as belonging to the world of sense, these actions must instead be understood as determined by other appearances, namely by desires and inclinations. If I were solely a member of the world of understanding, all my actions would therefore conform perfectly with the principle of autonomy of the pure will; if I were solely an item in the world of sense, they would have to be taken to conform perfectly with the natural law of desires and inclinations, and hence with the heteronomy of nature. (The former would rest on the supreme principle of morality, the latter on that of happiness.) But since *the world of the understanding contains the ground of the world of sense, and hence also of its laws*, it is thus immediately legislating with regard to my will (which belongs wholly to the world of understanding), and must be conceived of in this way. Thus as an intelligence, 454 although I recognize myself on the one hand as a being belonging to the world of sense, I also recognize myself as subject to the laws of the world of understanding—i.e. the world of reason, which contains its law in the idea of freedom, and thus in the autonomy of the will. Consequently I must view the laws of the world of the understanding as imperatives for me, and actions that conform with this principle as duties.

And thus categorical imperatives are possible because of this: the idea of freedom makes me a member of an intelligible world. As a result, if I were only that, all my actions *would* always conform with the autonomy of the will; but because I also perceive myself to be a member of the world of sense, they *ought* to conform with it. And this *categorical* ought represents a synthetic a priori proposition, because to my will affected by sensuous desires there is added the idea of the same will, but belonging to the world of the understanding, pure and practical by itself, which according to reason contains the supreme condition of the former. This roughly resembles the way in which the concepts of the understanding, which by themselves signify nothing but the form of law as such, are added to the intuitions of the world of sense, and thereby make possible synthetic a priori propositions, on which all knowledge of nature is based.

The practical use of common human reason confirms the correctness of this deduction. There is no one, not even the most wicked villain who—as long as they are otherwise accustomed to using reason—does not, when faced with examples of honesty of purpose, of steadfastness in following good maxims, and of sympathy and general benevolence involving great sacrifices of advantage and comfort, wish that they too might be so disposed. But because of their inclinations and impulses they find this hard to bring about in themselves; as a result, they wish to be free of such inclinations, which they themselves find burdensome. In this way they prove that with a will free from impulses of sensibility, they transfer themselves in thought into an order of things altogether different from that of their desires in the field of sensibility. For they cannot expect that the fulfilment of their wish will gratify their desires, or satisfy any of their actual or even conceivable inclinations (as this would rob the idea behind the wish of its pre-eminence). All they can expect is a greater inner worth of their person. But they believe themselves to be this better person when 455 they transfer themselves to the standpoint of a member of the world of the understanding. Without their choosing, this is what the idea of freedom, namely independence from *determining* causes of the world of sense, necessitates them to do. From here, they are conscious of possessing a good will which by their own admission constitutes the law for their evil will (which they possess as a member of the world of sense); and they acknowledge the eminence of this law even as they transgress it. The moral 'I ought' is thus one's own necessary 'I will' as a member of the intelligible world; and a person thinks of it as an *ought* only insofar as they consider themselves at the same time as a member of the world of sense.

Of the outermost boundary of all practical philosophy*

All human beings think of themselves as having a will that is free; because of this we judge of actions that they *ought* to have been done, even if they *were not done*. But this freedom is not an empirical concept; and nor can it be one, since the will remains even though experience seems to contradict those demands which are to be thought of as necessary once freedom is presupposed. On the other hand, it is equally necessary that everything that happens be inexorably determined according to laws of nature; and this natural necessity is no experiential concept either, precisely because it involves the concept of necessity, and therefore of a priori knowledge. But this way of conceiving nature is confirmed by experience and must unavoidably be presupposed if experience—namely knowledge of objects of the senses that cohere according to universal laws—is to be possible. That is why freedom is only an *idea* of reason, the objective reality of which is in itself doubtful, whereas nature is *a concept of the understanding* which proves, and must necessarily prove, its reality in examples taken from experience.

From this there arises a dialectic of reason: the freedom ascribed to the will seems to be in contradiction with natural necessity. At this parting of the ways, reason finds the route of natural necessity much more even and useful than that of freedom for *speculative purposes*; but when it comes to *practical purposes*, it is only on the footpath of 456 freedom that it is possible to make use of reason in our conduct. As a result, it is impossible for either the subtlest philosophy or the commonest human reason to rationalize freedom away. We must therefore presuppose that no true contradiction can be found between the presence of *both* freedom and natural necessity in human actions, as it cannot give up the concept of nature any more than that of freedom.

Nevertheless, even if we were never able to comprehend how freedom is possible, this apparent contradiction needs to be eliminated convincingly. For if the very thought of freedom contradicts itself, or contradicts the thought of nature (which is equally necessary), freedom would have to be given up altogether in favour of natural necessity.

But this contradiction would be unavoidable if the subject who deems themselves free were to think of themselves *in the same sense*, or *in just the same relation* when they call themselves free, and when with regard to the same action they take themselves to be subject to the law of nature. That is why speculative philosophy has this indispensable task: to show at the very least that it falls into this deception regarding the contradiction because we think of a human being differently and in a different relation when we call them free, from when we take them, as a piece of nature, to be subject to its laws. And both not only *can* coexist very well, but also *must* be thought of *as necessarily united* in the same subject, as otherwise there would be no call to burden reason with an idea of this sort: for even if this idea can be united *without contradiction* with another idea that has been adequately justified, it still entangles us in a business that puts reason in its theoretical use into a very tight bind. However, this duty falls on speculative philosophy solely that it may create a clear path for practical philosophy. It is therefore not just left to the philosopher's discretion to remove the seeming conflict, or leave it untouched. For if they opt for the latter, this leaves a no man's land which the fatalist is in their rights to occupy, and can then chase all of morality out of its supposed property, which it would have no title to hold.

Nevertheless, it cannot be said that the boundary of practical philosophy begins at this point. For the settlement of this dispute does not belong to practical philosophy at all; practical philosophy merely requires speculative reason to put an end to the discord in which reason entangles itself in theoretical questions, so that practical 457 reason may have peace and security from external attacks that would contest the ground on which it wants to settle.

The legitimate claim made by even common human reason to freedom of the will is based on the consciousness and accepted presupposition of reason's independence from those merely subjective determining causes that together make up what merely belongs to sensation and comes under the general name of sensibility. A human being in this way thinks of themselves as an intelligence. Thinking of themselves as an intelligence endowed with a will, and thus causality, they put themselves into a different order of things and in relation to determining grounds of a completely different sort, to when they perceive themselves as a phenomenon in the world of sense (which they actually are as well) and their causality as subject to external determination under laws of nature. Now, they soon become aware that both can, and indeed must, take place together. For there is not the slightest contradiction in a *thing in appearance* (belonging to the world of sense) being subject to certain laws from which, *as a thing* or a being *in itself*, it is independent. That they must represent and think of themselves in this twofold way is due, firstly, to the consciousness of themselves as an object affected by the senses, and secondly, to the consciousness of themselves as an intelligence—that is, as independent of sensible impressions in its use of reason, and hence as belonging to the world of understanding.

That is why a human being claims to have a will which cannot have imputed to it anything pertaining merely to their desires and inclinations; and why on the contrary, they attribute to themselves the possibility—indeed the necessity—of actions which disregard all desires and inducements of sense. The cause of such actions lies in themselves as an intelligence, and in the laws of effects and actions according to the principles of an intelligible world. Of that world, they may well only know that reason alone, and indeed pure reason independently of sensibility, is the source of its laws. Moreover, since in that world, as an intelligence only, they are properly themselves (whereas as a human being they are the appearance of themselves), those laws concern them immediately and categorically. Thus, whatever desires and impulses, and hence the whole nature of the sensible 458 world, may incite them to do cannot infringe on their will as an intelligence. Indeed, they do not answer for such desires and impulses, or attribute them to their true self, i.e. to their will; though, if they were to let them influence their maxims to the detriment of the rational laws governing their will, they would attribute to themselves their indulgence of those desires and impulses.

By *thinking* itself into a world of understanding, practical reason does not overstep its boundary in the least; as it would if it wanted to *intuit* or *feel* its way into it. This thinking amounts only to a negative thought, namely that the world of sense gives no laws to reason in its determining of the will, and its only positive point is this: that the negative characteristic of freedom is combined with a (positive) capacity and even with a causality of reason, which we call a will—the capacity to act so that the principle of our actions conforms with the essential feature of a rational cause, namely that the maxim of these actions have the universal validity of a law. But if in addition it were to fetch an *object of the will*, i.e. a motive, from the world of understanding, then practical reason would indeed overstep its bounds, in presuming an acquaintance with something of which it knows nothing. The concept of a world of understanding is thus only a *standpoint* outside appearances that reason sees itself as required to take, *in order to think of itself as practical*. This would not be possible if the influences of sensibility determined a human being; yet it is required insofar as they are not to be denied consciousness of themselves as an intelligence, and hence as a rational cause active through reason, and so as operating freely. Of course, this thought leads on to the idea of an order and form of legislation that is distinct from that of the mechanism of nature, which is what governs the world of sense. The concept of an intelligible world (i.e. of the totality of rational beings, as things in themselves) is thereby made necessary, but without in the least presuming to think of such a world in anything other than *formal terms*—that is, as conforming to the condition that the maxim of the will has the universality of a law, and so conforming to the autonomy of the will, which alone is consistent with freedom. By contrast, all laws which are determined by reference to an object result in heteronomy, which can be found only in laws of nature and can apply only to the laws of sense.

But reason would overstep all its bounds if it ventured to *explain how* pure reason can be practical, which would be the same as explaining *how freedom is possible*. 459

For the only way we can explain something is by tracing it back to laws whose object can be given in possible experience. But freedom is a mere idea, whose objective reality in line with laws of nature, or in any possible experience, can in no way be established. It can thus never be comprehended or even just looked into, since no underpinning analogous example of it could ever be found. It holds only as a necessary presupposition of reason in a being that believes itself to be conscious of possessing a will, that is to say a capacity—distinct from a mere faculty of desire—to determine itself to act as an intelligence and therefore according to laws of reason, independent of natural instinct. But where determination by laws of nature comes to an end, all *explanation* comes to an end as well. All that remains is *defence*, i.e. warding off objections from those who pretend to have looked more deeply into the essence of things, and as a result boldly declare that freedom is impossible. All that can be done is to show them how the contradiction they have supposedly discovered simply lies in this: in order to make the law of nature hold with regard to human actions, they necessarily had to view the human being as an appearance; and now, in also taking him as an intelligent being, they must think of him as a thing in itself, while continuing to view him as an appearance. As a result, it is of course the case that a contradiction would arise if, in one and the same subject, his causality (i.e. of his will) were hived off from all natural laws of the world of sense. But this contradiction vanishes once the objector is willing to reflect and grant, as is fair, that behind the appearances there must lie at their foundation the way things are in themselves* (although hidden), and that it cannot be expected that the laws by which they operate should be one and the same as those under which their appearances are governed.

The subjective impossibility of *explaining* freedom of the will is just the same as the impossibility of finding and making it comprehensible that a human being could take an *interest*[1] in moral laws; and yet they really do take such an interest, the basis of which we call 'moral feeling'. Some have mistakenly taken this to be the standard for our moral judgement; but it ought rather to be regarded as the

---

[1] An interest is that through which reason becomes practical—that is, becomes a cause determining the will. This is why it is only said of a rational being that it takes an interest in something; non-rational creatures feel only sensuous impulses. Reason takes an immediate interest in an action only when the universal validity of its maxim is a ground that is sufficient to determine the will. Only such an interest is pure. If reason is only able to motivate the will by means of some further object of desire, or under the presupposition of a special feeling of the subject, then it takes only a mediated interest in the action. And the latter interest would be merely empirical, and not a pure rational interest, since reason all by itself, without the help of experience, is unable to discover objects of the will or a special feeling underlying the will. The logical interest that belongs to reason, of expanding its insight, is never immediate, but rather presupposes some purpose.

subjective effect exercised on our will by the law, for which reason
alone supplies the objective grounds.

It is admittedly required that reason should have a power of *inspir-
ing* a *feeling of pleasure* or of delight in fulfilling duty, in order to will
the actions that it by itself prescribes to a sensuously affected being as
what ought to be done; and hence reason has a causal capacity to
determine that sensibility conform to principles. However, it is completely impossible to understand (i.e. to make comprehensible a priori) how a mere thought, which itself contains nothing sensuous, can
produce a sensation of pleasure or displeasure. For that is a special
kind of causality about which, as about any causality, we can determine nothing whatsoever a priori, but must consult experience alone.
But experience cannot offer us a relation of cause and effect except
between two objects of experience—whereas here pure reason through
mere ideas (which provide no object for experience) has to be the
cause of an effect which is nonetheless to be found in experience.
Hence for us human beings, it is quite impossible to explain how and
why the *universality of a maxim as a law*, and hence morality, interests
us. Only this is certain: it is not *because the law interests us* that it
has validity for us. For this would be heteronomy and would make
practical reason dependent on sensibility, namely on an underlying 461
feeling, in which case practical reason could never be a source of
moral legislation. Rather, the law interests us because it is valid for us
as human beings, since it originates from our will as an intelligence,
hence from our actual self. *But what belongs to mere appearance is
necessarily subordinated by reason to the way things are in themselves.**

Thus the question 'how is a categorical imperative possible?' can
be answered to the extent that one can state the one presupposition
that makes it possible, which is the idea of freedom, and likewise we
can see that this presupposition is necessary. This is sufficient for the
practical use of reason, i.e. to convince us that the imperative and the
moral law is *valid*, even though human reason cannot ever understand how this presupposition is itself possible. Nonetheless, on the
presupposition that the will of an intelligence is free, its *autonomy*
follows necessarily as the formal condition under which alone such
a will can be determined. Presupposing this freedom of the will is not
only perfectly *possible* (as speculative philosophy can show, and without

contradicting the principle that appearances in the world of sense are governed by natural necessity); it is also unconditionally *necessary* for a rational being—conscious of its causality through reason, and hence of a will (different from desires)—to suppose it practically, that is, in the idea involved in all the actions it chooses, as their condition. But human reason is totally incapable of explaining *how* pure reason, without any other drives from anywhere else, can by itself be practical. That is, it cannot explain how the mere *principle of the universal validity of all its maxims as laws* (which of course is the form of a pure practical reason) can by itself yield a drive and produce an interest that can be called purely *moral*, without any matter (i.e. object) of the will in which one could take some prior interest. In other words, human reason cannot explain *how pure reason can be practical*; and all the effort and labour spent in seeking an explanation for it are wasted.

Precisely the same would hold if I attempted to fathom how freedom itself as the causality of the will is possible. For then I would take

462 leave of philosophy as the basis of explanation; and I have no other. I might indeed swan around* in the intelligible world, the world of intelligences—that is still open to me. But while I may have a well-founded *idea* of such a thing, I have not the least *acquaintance* with it, and nor could I achieve such acquaintance despite all the efforts of my natural powers of reason.

All my *idea* signifies is a who-knows-what that is left over when I have excluded everything that belongs to the world of the senses from the determining grounds of my will. I do this in order to restrict the principle of motives which arise from the field of sensibility by setting its bounds, to show that this field does not encompass everything, and that there is still more beyond it; but with this 'more' I am no further acquainted. After hiving off all matter, i.e. all knowledge of objects, nothing is left to me of pure reason—which thinks of this ideal—except the form, namely, the practical law of the universality of maxims, and, as a result, the conception of reason as a possible efficient cause in relation to a pure world of the understanding, i.e. one determining the will. The cause could not be a drive; if it were, it would have to be this idea of the intelligible world itself, or that in which reason originally takes an interest—but this is precisely the thing we cannot understand.

Here, then, is the supreme boundary of all moral inquiry. To identify this is of the greatest importance, so that reason neither, on the
one hand, and to the detriment of morals, goes looking in the world of
sense for the supreme motive, and a comprehensible but empirical
interest; nor on the other, loses herself among phantasms, impotently
and, without actually moving, flapping her wings in the space—empty
for her—of transcendent ideas, under the name of the intelligible
world. The idea of a pure world of the understanding, as a totality of
all intelligences, to which we ourselves as rational beings belong
(albeit that on the other hand we are just as much members of the
world of sense), always remains a useful and permissible idea within
a rational faith—in order to give us a lively interest in the moral law
through the glorious ideal of a universal kingdom of ends in themselves (rational beings), to which we can belong as members if we
carefully follow maxims of freedom as though they were laws of 463
nature—even if all knowledge ends at its border.

Concluding Remark

With regards to nature, the speculative use of reason leads to the absolute necessity of some supreme cause of *the world*; *in respect of freedom*, the practical use of reason also leads to absolute necessity, but
only of *laws of action* for a rational being as such. Now it is an essential
principle of all uses of our reason to drive its knowledge through to the
point at which we are conscious of its *necessity*—for otherwise this
knowledge would not belong to reason. But it is an equally essential
limitation of the very same reason that it cannot *understand* the necessity, either of what is, what happens, or what ought to happen, unless
a *condition* can be found as the basis on which it is, or happens or
ought to happen. However, the result of constantly inquiring into the
nature of this condition is that the satisfaction of reason is just postponed again and again. Reason therefore restlessly seeks the *unconditionally* necessary, and finds itself required to presuppose such a thing
without having any means to comprehend it; just to find the concept
that is compatible with this presupposition is fortune enough. Our
deduction of the supreme principle of morality has thus been unable
to make it comprehensible that an unconditional practical law (which is

what the categorical imperative must be) can be absolutely necessary—
but this is no criticism, as the same charge would have to be directed
at human reason as such. For it cannot count against our deduction
that it does not seek to make such necessity comprehensible by giving
a condition, namely by means of finding its basis in some interest;
there would then be no morality, i.e. no supreme law of freedom.
Thus although we do not comprehend the unconditional practical
necessity of the moral imperative, we do comprehend its *incomprehensibility*; and this is all that can reasonably be demanded of a philosophy whose principles strive to reach the very boundary of human
reason.

EXPLANATORY NOTES

NOTE: References to the majority of Kant's texts are to the volume and page number of the Akademie edition of Kant's works, which can be found in the margins of most English translations. The exception is references to the *Critique of Pure Reason*, which are based on the pagination of the first (A) edition and second (B) edition, which again can usually be found in the margin of translations of this text.

PREFACE

3 *philosophy which is based on experience ... called pure*: 'a priori' is a common term in philosophy, and typically means independent of, or prior to, experience. It is usually contrasted with a posteriori (see below).

4 *practical anthropology*: Kant gave lectures on anthropology from 1772 to 1796, and his *Anthropology from a Pragmatic Point of View* was published in 1798. In this work he defines anthropology as 'A doctrine of the knowledge of the human being, systematically formulated'. He distinguishes between physiological knowledge of the human being, which 'concerns what *nature* makes of the human being', and pragmatic knowledge concerning what a free being can and should make of themselves (7:119).

moral theory: the German here is 'Moral', a now outdated term, which describes the *study* of morality, rather then directly referring to morality itself.

5 *non-moral*: the German here is 'der unsittliche Grund'. Timmermann suggests (see Gregor and Timmermann 2011, 162) that 'immoral' is a better translation, as Kant uses the term more pejoratively elsewhere, while also holding that Kant rejects moral indifferents, so that what is not moral is therefore then immoral. In this context, however, we think a more neutral meaning is acceptable and more natural.

6 *Wolff*: a reference to Christian Wolff (1679–1754), the most eminent German philosopher between Leibniz and Kant, and who was widely influential at this time.

'*universal practical philosophy*': this is a reference to Wolff's *Philosophia practica universalis*, which was published in Latin in 1738–9, and then elaborated in a German version by Georg Friedrich Meier under the title *Allgemeine praktische Weltweisheit* in 1764.

willing in general: in common-sense terms, as when we are thinking about having a 'strong' or 'iron' will, or being 'weak willed', or having 'free will', the will is the capacity for action, decision, and choice. Rather than seeing the will as separate from reason and emotion, and as something that chooses between the two of them, Kant identifies the will with reason in its practical form. In later work, however, he goes on to complicate this picture, when he distinguishes the will as practical reason (*Wille*) from the capacity for free choice (*Willkür*), while nevertheless insisting that both of them are aspects of the will: see *The Metaphysics of Morals* 6:213–14.

6 *a posteriori*: a posteriori is the contrast to a priori, and means from or after experience. Kant uses these terms here to distinguish between the two possible origins of our concepts, though they can also refer to two kinds of justification or knowledge of propositions, and whether this justification or knowledge comes from experience or without recourse to experience.

Intending some day...Metaphysics of Morals: in the following decade (1797), Kant went on to publish his *Metaphysics of Morals*, covering legal and political philosophy (the 'Doctrine of Right') and ethics ('the 'Doctrine of Virtue'), in which he attempts to derive more concrete conclusions about morality. Although the title *Metaphysics of Morals* might suggest that he uses the framework developed in the *Groundwork*, the relation between these two texts is not entirely straightforward, in part given further developments in Kant's thinking in the intervening period.

Groundwork: while 'foundation' might be the more straightforward English translation of '*Grundlegung*', we have stuck with the convention of translating it as 'Groundwork', as this is now standardly used in translations and commentaries. It should be noted, however, that in the next sentence, Kant uses the term 'Grundlage' which we translate as 'foundation'. There is therefore a play on words in German, where 'Grundlegung' means the activity of laying foundations or groundworks, while 'Grundlage' refers to the foundations or groundworks themselves.

Critique of a pure practical reason: three years after the publication of the *Groundwork*, Kant published the *Critique of Practical Reason* (1788). This work covers some similar ground, and there is a scholarly dispute about the extent to which it represents an extension of Kant's thoughts in the *Groundwork*, or a break with it.

7 *Critique of pure theoretical reason...published*: this is a reference to Kant's *Critique of Pure Reason*, published in its first edition in 1781, and in a second edition in 1787. This work began the so-called 'critical project' of Kant's mature philosophy, which approaches metaphysics by attempting to map and set boundaries to the capacities of rational inquiry, in a self-reflective and therefore critical manner. The aim is to prevent metaphysics exceeding those boundaries and engaging in unresolvable speculative debates in matters that extend beyond possible experience. This becomes an issue that Kant deals with in Section III of the *Groundwork*.

· *analytically... and back again synthetically*: this appears to be a distinction between two types of method that relates to Kant's famous distinction between analytic and synthetic propositions. For further discussion of the distinction, see note below relating to p. 31, on p. 81, and our Introduction.

SECTION I

9 *happiness*: while this is the usual translation for 'Glückseligkeit', Kant has something more substantive in mind than is now often meant by the term in English. It is the German equivalent of the Latin *beautitudo*, with connotations of felicity or blessedness, or even bliss. A few pages later, Kant defines happiness as 'the idea that all inclinations are satisfied together' (4:399).

10 *organs*: 'Werkzeug' would normally be translated as 'tool' or 'instrument', but as Timmermann (see Gregor and Timmermann 2011, 163) points out, it is best translated as 'organ' in this context: 'As the etymology of the word indicates, organs are instruments employed by an organism for its various tasks.'

11 *common luxury*: here, Kant is likely referring to the luxury debate of the eighteenth century, where the arts and sciences had been criticized by Rousseau as mere luxuries.

15 *second proposition*: Kant never explicitly tells the reader what the first proposition is. Some interpretation is therefore needed at this point. We suggest in the Introduction that the first proposition should be read as Kant's claim that a properly dutiful person, who has real moral worth, is one who acts *from* duty, and not from an inclination that is merely *in accordance with* duty (cf. 4:397–9).

drivers: '*Triebfeder*' has often been translated as 'incentive'. However, a *Triebfeder* is the driving spring of a mechanism, such as a watch or mechanical toy, and we have therefore opted to translate it as 'drive' or 'driver'.

16 *respect for the law*: the German term here is 'Achtung', which as well as meaning respect has implications of reverence and awe, and therefore involves elements of attraction and deference.

20 *natural dialectic*: 'dialectic' was a term used prior to Kant to refer to the back and forth of argument that progresses through opposition. Kant is building on this idea, but thinks that reason (in particular) can generate contradictions that are irresolvable, which then need diagnosis or critique, rather than futile assertion and counter-assertion. Therefore here, Kant's point is that without the approach he will develop in what follows, reason can get stuck in an oscillation between asserting its moral authority and questioning it at one and the same time.

SECTION II

22 *what counts... which one does not*: Cf. 2 Corinthians 4:18: 'While we look
not at the things which are seen, but at the things which are not seen: for
things that are seen are temporal; but the things which are not seen are
eternal'.

23 *'Why do you call... do not see'*: cf. Luke 18:19, Matthew 19:17, Mark 10:18.

24 *popular practical philosophy*: a reference to a group of German Enlighten-
ment philosophers of Kant's time whose main representative for Kant was
Christian Garve (1742–98), who published a notorious review of the
Critique of Pure Reason. Letters from J. G. Hamann (1730–88) suggest that
the *Groundwork* began as an attack on Garve's translation and commentary
on Cicero's *De Officiis*.

25 *admirable late Professor Sulzer*: the Swiss aesthetician and natural philosopher Johann Georg Sulzer (1720–79), who translated David Hume's
Enquiry Concerning the Principles of Morals into German. There is some
dispute about whether the precise letter referred to here is to be found in
the extant correspondence between the two men.

26 *ideas*: Kant has a specific conception of ideas (*Ideen*), which are concepts
that go beyond all possible experience. He develops this in the *Critique of
Pure Reason*, where he tells us the following: 'A concept is either an empirical or a pure concept, and the pure concept, insofar as it has its origin
solely in the understanding (not in a pure image of sensibility), is called
notion. A concept made up of notions, which goes beyond the possibility
of experience, is an idea or a concept of reason' (A320/B377).

28 *would represent*: the use of 'would' here suggests there is some uncertainty
as to whether categorical imperatives actually can do this. This is something that Kant will leave unresolved in this section, but turn to address in
Section III.

29 *problematically ... assertorically ... apodictically practical principle*: by
a *problematic* principle, Kant means a principle that declares that an action
is good for some end or purpose that we *might or might not* happen to have,
the validity of which is therefore conditional. By an *assertorical* principle,
Kant means a principle that declares that an action is good for some end
or purpose that we *actually* have, and which therefore is actually valid for
us, even though it might not have been; and by an *apodictically practical
principle*, Kant means a principle that declares that an action is necessary
without reference to any purpose or end of ours, the validity of which is therefore necessary. Kant also uses this terminology in the *Critique of Pure
Reason* A74–5/B100–1.

31 *how are all these imperatives possible?*: this way of posing a question, by
asking how it is even possible that something is the case, is characteristic
of Kant, where in his *Prolegomena to Any Future Metaphysics*, he calls these

'transcendental questions': see 4:279–80. See also the *Critique of Pure Reason*, B19–24.

When it comes to the will, this proposition is analytic: in the *Critique of Pure Reason*, Kant distinguishes between *analytic* and *synthetic* propositions. In many propositions, we attribute a property to a subject, such as 'This tomato [subject] is ripe [property]'. Analytic propositions are those in which the property attributed to the subject is already contained in the very concept of that subject. For instance, 'A triangle has three angles' is analytic, since it is simply what is meant by 'triangle' that it has three angles. For this reason analytic propositions help us better understand the nature of our concepts and their interrelations, but do not typically tell us about the world. Synthetic propositions, by contrast, do tell us about the world by ascribing some property to a subject that is not contained in its very concept—for instance, 'The grass on my lawn is overgrown' or 'This tomato is ripe'. For further discussion of Kant's distinctions here, see the note on a priori synthetic propositions below.

34 *It is an a priori synthetic practical proposition*: it seemed to Kant that there must be synthetic a priori propositions, such as 'every event has a cause', which cannot be generalizations from experience, but are also not known to be true by mere analysis of the concepts involved. However, these propositions are problematic: how can a proposition both be synthetic (telling us something about the world) and a priori (known independently of experience of the world)? This is why Kant says here that it is 'difficult to make sense of the possibility of such propositions when it comes to theoretical knowledge'. Kant developed his transcendental idealism to explain how such propositions are possible (see the Introduction to the *Critique of Pure Reason*), arguing that such propositions apply to the framework of all our possible experience and thus to everything in experience, while knowledge of this framework is a priori. In addition, Kant notes in this passage that practical philosophy also involves propositions which cannot be thought of as either analytic or a posteriori, thus posing a challenge which is analogous to the one facing theoretical philosophy, and which he also attempts to address in Section III using ideas from transcendental idealism. See our Introduction for further discussion.

35 *also*: the German here is 'zugleich', which can also be translated as 'at the same time', but this is potentially misleading, as it suggests that holding two ideas in mind simultaneously is where the test lies. The non-temporal reading is clear in the initial statement of the universal law test at 4:402, where 'auch' ('also') instead of 'zugleich' is used. We have adopted the same translation in subsequent variants of the categorical imperative.

I here understand . . . to ground an exception: this is a puzzling claim for Kant to make, as it suggests that we are allowed to make exceptions to imperfect duties based upon our inclinations. In his later *Metaphysics of Morals*,

Kant seems to clarify this, when he claims that 'a wide duty is not to be understood as a permission to make exceptions to the maxim of actions, but only as one to limit one obligatory maxim by another (e.g. general love of one's neighbour by the love of one's parents), by which the field for the practice of virtue is indeed widened' (6:390).

38 *strict or narrower (inflexible) duty... wider (meritorious) duty*: here Kant is using a traditional distinction between duties that are perfect or strict on the one hand and imperfect or wide on the other. The distinction turns on the degree of latitude that is allowed to the agent, from none in the case of strict duties, and some in the case of wider duties. What this latitude involves is not entirely clear, but it may be such as to allow the agent discretion in how to comply with the duty, or allow exceptions, or make the action merely virtuous rather than strictly required. Kant develops these distinctions more fully in the *Metaphysics of Morals* 6:390–1.

40 *Juno*: a reference to a Greek myth, in which the king Ixion is deceived by Jupiter into attempting to make love to a cloud, which he takes to be Jupiter's wife, Juno.

42 *final section*: this seems to refer to the second subsection of Section III (4:447–8), where Kant argues that freedom must be presupposed as a property of the will of all rational beings.

43 *all of its actions*: by *all* here, Kant refers to actions directed towards oneself *and* others (cf. 4:428).

Here I must forgo the more precise account: we arguably find this detail in Kant's later work, *The Metaphysics of Morals*.

46 *kingdom*: following convention, we translate 'Reich' as 'kingdom' rather than 'empire' or 'realm'.

48 *purposeless play of the powers of our mind*: this relates to Kant's views on aesthetics, which he goes on to explore in the *Critique of Judgement* (1790). There, he argues that judgements of beauty do not involve applying a concept or purpose to their object. Instead, they are the free play of the imagination and understanding, which gives rise to a distinctive feeling of pleasure.

aesthetic price: other translators use 'fancy price' for 'Affectionspreiss', where we have opted for 'aesthetic price'. Of course, neither is a common term in English, but Kant's basic idea seems to be that this kind of 'price' or valuation is based on the purposeless play of the faculties of the mind that he associates with aesthetic judgement, which is why we have opted for our translation.

53 *business of the present section*: once more, Kant is putting off a critique of the subject until Section III.

54 *subjected to critique*: with this, Kant is pointing back to the work he has accomplished in the *Critique of Pure Reason*, but also perhaps pointing

forward to the work he will undertake in the final section of the *Groundwork*, which he calls 'Transition from the Metaphysics of Morals to the Critique of Pure Practical Reason'.

All principles... our will: Kant elaborates on this distinction, and identifies individual representatives of the various positions discussed, in the *Critique of Practical Reason*, 5:40–1. Happiness based on physical feeling is associated with the hedonism of Epicurus (341–270 BC); happiness based on moral feeling is associated with the moral sense theory of Francis Hutcheson (1694–1727); the rational principle of perfection is associated with Christian Wolff and the Stoics; and the rationalist divine command morality is associated with Christian August Crucius (1715–75).

SECTION III

60 *the latter is always a synthetic proposition*: this is a notoriously difficult sentence. It is problematic in more than one way. Firstly, what exactly is Kant referring to by 'the latter'? The content of the preceding sentence (to which 'latter' would seem to refer) suggests that it could be 'morality and its principle'. However, the structure of the sentence as it proceeds suggests that the 'latter' is instead 'an absolutely good will is that whose maxim, when considered as a universal law, can always be contained within itself'. But then secondly, it is not clear why either claim would be *synthetic*. For 'morality and its principle' is not even a proposition; while Kant seems to have developed *analytical* connections between the good will and the formula of universal law in Section I of the *Groundwork*. For further discussion, see our Introduction.

62 *'I ought' is actually an 'I will'*: in German, this rhymes: 'dieses Sollen ist eigentlich ein Wollen'.

63 *equivalent concepts*: 'Wechselbegriffe' has often been rendered by other translators as 'reciprocal concepts', but it is more straightforward to say that these two concepts are equivalent, since 'reciprocity' has the distracting connotation that they involve some kind of mutuality. We should note, however, that Kant also refers to this idea in Latin as *conceptus reciproci* in his lectures on logic (e.g. 9:98; 24:755), though the context makes it clear that the meaning is not 'reciprocal', so that the translators of these texts have used 'convertible' for 'reciproci'.

63 *things in themselves*: Kant is here building on ideas developed further in the *Critique of Pure Reason*: see Bxv–xxii, A26–30/B42–6, A32–49/B49–73, A235–60/B294–315, A490–7/B518–25. See also our Introduction.

64 *reason... the understanding in this respect*: Kant has a distinctive conception of reason and the understanding, which he develops in the *Critique of Pure Reason*. The understanding is involved in our judgements based on

experience and which therefore concern the empirical world, whereas reason goes beyond experience. It is thus less tied to *receptivity* (i.e. what the mind receives from experience) and so is characterized here in terms of a pure *spontaneity* (i.e. the mind's activity independent of experience).

65 *ideas*: as noted earlier (p. 80), Kant conceives of ideas in a special way, namely as concepts that go beyond all possible experience.

68 *outermost boundary*: in the *Prolegomena to any Future Metaphysics* (1783), Kant distinguishes between *boundaries* (Grenzen) and *limits* (Schranken) —see 4:352. Boundaries require a space on the other side of them that helps set the boundary, whereas limits do not. While Kant does not deploy the distinction in an explicit way in the *Groundwork*, it is important for his thought. Our experience, for instance, has limits, but not boundaries; there is no *space* outside our experience, but our experience isn't everything.

72 *the way things are in themselves*: Kant uses 'die Sachen an sich selbst' here, rather than the phrase he uses more frequently in the *Critique of Pure Reason*, which is 'Dinge an sich selbst'.

73 *the way things are in themselves*: once more, Kant uses the term 'Sache'.

74 *swan around*: 'Schwärmen' has connotations of irrational enthusiasm or fanaticism, as in *Schwärmerei*.

GLOSSARY

This German–English glossary lists certain words that can be problematic to translate into English, to make clear which options we have chosen or where we have used a range of alternatives. For a full glossary of terms from the *Groundwork* compiled by Stephen Orr, see http://groundlaying. appspot.com/html/gms_master_glossar.html#glossarE.

die **Achtung** respect
allgemein general, universal, common
das **Begehrungsvermögen** faculty of desire
die **Bestimmung** determination, feature, account, characteristic
der **Bewegungsgrund** motive, motivating ground, ground
der **Bösewicht** villain
die **Empfindung** feeling, sensation
die **Erkenntnis** knowledge (cognition)
das **Geschäft** trade, business, project, vocation
die **Grenze** boundary
die **Lehre** teachings, doctrines

die **Naturlehre** natural philosophy, investigation of nature
die **Nötigung** necessitation
das **Reich** kingdom
die **Seelenlehre** psychology
die **Sittenlehre** doctrine of morals, moral theory
die **Triebfeder** drive/driver
das **Vermögen** faculty, capacity
die **Vorstellung** representation
die **Wechselbegriff** equivalent concept
die **Wirklichkeit** reality
das **Wissen** knowledge
die **Wohltat** beneficence
das **Wohlwollen** benevolence
die **Würde** dignity
der **Zweck** end/purpose

INDEX

The Oxford World's Classics Website

www.worldsclassics.co.uk

- Browse the full range of Oxford World's Classics online

- Sign up for our monthly e-alert to receive information on new titles

- Read extracts from the Introductions

- Listen to our editors and translators talk about the world's greatest literature with our Oxford World's Classics audio guides

- Join the conversation, follow us on Twitter at OWC_Oxford

- Teachers and lecturers can order inspection copies quickly and simply via our website

www.worldsclassics.co.uk

American Literature

British and Irish Literature

Children's Literature

Classics and Ancient Literature

Colonial Literature

Eastern Literature

European Literature

Gothic Literature

History

Medieval Literature

Oxford English Drama

Philosophy

Poetry

Politics

Religion

The Oxford Shakespeare

A complete list of Oxford World's Classics, including Authors in Context, Oxford English Drama, and the Oxford Shakespeare, is available in the UK from the Marketing Services Department, Oxford University Press, Great Clarendon Street, Oxford OX2 6DP, or visit the website at www.oup.com/uk/worldsclassics.

In the USA, visit www.oup.com/us/owc for a complete title list.

Oxford World's Classics are available from all good bookshops. In case of difficulty, customers in the UK should contact Oxford University Press Bookshop, 116 High Street, Oxford OX1 4BR.

Classical Literary Criticism
The First Philosophers: The Presocrats
  and the Sophists
Greek Lyric Poetry
Myths from Mesopotamia

APOLLODORUS   The Library of Greek Mythology

APOLLONIUS OF RHODES   Jason and the Golden Fleece

APULEIUS   The Golden Ass

ARISTOPHANES   Birds and Other Plays

ARISTOTLE   The Nicomachean Ethics
Politics

ARRIAN   Alexander the Great

BOETHIUS   The Consolation of Philosophy

CAESAR   The Civil War
The Gallic War

CATULLUS   The Poems of Catullus

CICERO   Defence Speeches
The Nature of the Gods
On Obligations
Political Speeches
The Republic and The Laws

EURIPIDES   Bacchae and Other Plays
Heracles and Other Plays
Medea and Other Plays
Orestes and Other Plays
The Trojan Women and Other Plays

HERODOTUS   The Histories

HOMER   The Iliad
The Odyssey

THOMAS AQUINAS	**Selected Philosophical Writings**
FRANCIS BACON	**The Major Works**
WALTER BAGEHOT	**The English Constitution**
GEORGE BERKELEY	**Principles of Human Knowledge and Three Dialogues**
EDMUND BURKE	**A Philosophical Enquiry into the Sublime and Beautiful**
	Reflections on the Revolution in France
CONFUCIUS	**The Analects**
RENÉ DESCARTES	**A Discourse on the Method**
	Meditations on First Philosophy
ÉMILE DURKHEIM	**The Elementary Forms of Religious Life**
FRIEDRICH ENGELS	**The Condition of the Working Class in England**
JAMES GEORGE FRAZER	**The Golden Bough**
SIGMUND FREUD	**The Interpretation of Dreams**
G. W. E. HEGEL	**Outlines of the Philosophy of Right**
THOMAS HOBBES	**Human Nature and De Corpore Politico**
	Leviathan
DAVID HUME	**An Enquiry concerning Human Understanding**
	Selected Essays
IMMANUEL KANT	**Critique of Judgement**
SØREN KIERKEGAARD	**Repetition and Philosophical Crumbs**
JOHN LOCKE	**An Essay concerning Human Understanding**

Bhagavad Gita

The Bible Authorized King James Version
With Apocrypha

The Book of Common Prayer

Dhammapada

The Gospels

The Koran

The Pañcatantra

The Sauptikaparvan (from the
Mahabharata)

The Tale of Sinuhe and Other Ancient
Egyptian Poems

The Qur'an

Upanisads

ANSELM OF CANTERBURY	The Major Works
THOMAS AQUINAS	Selected Philosophical Writings
AUGUSTINE	The Confessions
	On Christian Teaching
BEDE	The Ecclesiastical History
KĀLIDĀSA	The Recognition of Śakuntalā
LAOZI	Daodejing
RUMI	The Masnavi
ŚĀNTIDEVA	The Bodhicaryāvatāra

	An Anthology of Elizabethan Prose Fiction
	Early Modern Women's Writing
	Three Early Modern Utopias (Utopia; New Atlantis; The Isle of Pines)
FRANCIS BACON	Essays
	The Major Works
APHRA BEHN	Oroonoko and Other Writings
	The Rover and Other Plays
JOHN BUNYAN	Grace Abounding
	The Pilgrim's Progress
JOHN DONNE	The Major Works
	Selected Poetry
JOHN FOXE	Book of Martyrs
BEN JONSON	The Alchemist and Other Plays
	The Devil is an Ass and Other Plays
	Five Plays
JOHN MILTON	The Major Works
	Paradise Lost
	Selected Poetry
EARL OF ROCHESTER	Selected Poems
SIR PHILIP SIDNEY	The Old Arcadia
	The Major Works
SIR PHILIP and MARY SIDNEY	The Sidney Psalter
IZAAK WALTON	The Compleat Angler